DON'T JUST GIVE YOUR STUFF AWAY

Learn to Manage Your Heart, Mind, Body & Time for Better Relationships Today

by Princess Love Mills

DON'T JUST GIVE YOUR STUFF AWAY

Copyright © 2012 by Princess Love Mills

No part of this book may be reproduced in any form or by any electronic or mechanical means including photocopying, information storage and retrieval systems, without permission in writing from the author. The only exception is by a reviewer, who may quote short excerpts in critical articles and reviews.

ALL RIGHTS RESERVED

Editor: Adelaida Montanez
Book Designer: Audrey Calloway
Cover Design Artist: Steven Scott www.Sovereign-Pictures.com

All Scripture quotations, unless otherwise indicated, are taken from the Holy Bible, New International Version. (r) NIV. Copyright © 1973, 1978, 1990, 1984 by International Bible society. Used by permission of Zondervan. All rights reserved.

Published by Love Speaks Productions, LLC
www.LoveSpeaks2U.com
info@LoveSpeaks2U.com
Duluth, Georgia, USA

DON'T JUST GIVE YOUR STUFF AWAY:
Learn to Manage Your Heart, Mind, Body, & Time for Better Relationships Today

Names of individuals listed in the stories have been changed to protect the privacy of the individuals involved. The author nor the publisher is a medical doctor and is not giving any form of professional medical advice to any reader. Please consult with your physician for your medical concerns and treatments. Neither the publisher nor author will be liable or responsible for any loss or damage allegedly resulting from any information or suggestions of this book.

Self-Help - Women's Studies - Self-Esteem - Relationships

First Edition

ISBN-13: 978-0-615-74447-6
ISBN-10: 0-61574-447-8

DEDICATION

This book is dedicated to my daughters:
Chloe, Alicia, & Kalana,
and my daughters from other mothers:
Dezyre, Trinity, Morgan, Star, Adrianne, Arianna, Regina,
Kira, Levine, Troy, Maia, Hope, Bailey, Mariah, Braelyn, Leah, Myesha,
Greer, Sarah, and all young ladies, young and refined.
Live this live on purpose and in power by managing your stuff.

ACKNOWLEDGEMENTS

    Apart from my personal efforts, I am fully aware that the success of any project largely depends on the inspiration, encouragement and contributions of others. I take this opportunity to express my sincere gratitude to the people who have been instrumental in the successful completion of this project. First and foremost, I would like to thank the Holy Spirit for his tangible presence in my life through many amazing people. I gratefully acknowledge my aunt Elsie who planted the seed of this book, after allowing me to share one of my journal entries. At the end of my reading she emphatically declared, "That should become a book!" Caught up in her excitement, I immediately agreed with her even though I wasn't quite sure what she was talking about. As time passed, the seed she planted began to grow.

    Next I'd like to enthusiastically thank Audrey for her contributions as encourager and interior book designer. Our friendship is approaching 25 years and she is always in my corner regardless of distance and time. When I shared my manuscript with her, she did not want to put it down. Her feedback was timely and priceless and from the moment she read my first draft, she has been fully committed to assist me in any way possible. Also, I would like to thank my editor Adelaida who was a gift to me from a mutual friend. Adelaida represents God's favor for my life and this project. Our kindred spirits forged an instant connection as she read her own thoughts and words in my manuscript. I must also acknowledge and thank Bishop T. D. Jakes for being the man of God he is and for his iconic presence in my life. Even though I have never met him, he traveled with me through a dark season in my life and he still provides good company when I need it.

    I would also like to thank my mother Berta who convinced me at a very young age I could do anything I wanted to do, if I set my mind to do it. Mom thanks for believing in me and all of my dreams. I also thank my silent contributors who simply provided their unique version of love and support, my sisters Demetria, Valencia, and Artemis and all of my extended family near and far. And finally I graciously thank my daughter Chloe who endured the entire process as I transitioned through a gamut of emotions and circumstances.

Contents

Introduction 1

Part I: THE LISTS & RELATIONSHIP STORIES

1. What Is "Your Stuff"? 3
2. The Lists 9
   - The Unavailable Men List 10
   - The Non-Family Men List 11
   - The Man-Child Men List 11
   - The Off Limits Men List 12
   - The Not Ever Men List 12
   - The Dangerous Men List 12
   - The Toxic Friendship List 13
3. Unavailable Men 15
   - Parker 20
   - Grayson 25
   - Grayson Part II 30
   - Toby 33
   - My Advice 38
4. Non-Family Men 43
   - Preston 44
5. Man-Child Men 47
   - Sebastian 47
   - Porsche's Story 49
6. Off Limits Men 53
   - Lucia's Story 55
   - Jennifer's Pain 56
7. Not Ever Men 59
   - Rebecca 59
8. Dangerous Men 64
   - Grace Got Away 66
9. Toxic Friendships 70
   - Tanisha 70
   - Jezzie 71
   - Friends at Work 72

Part II: CORE BELIEFS & BOUNDARIES

10 Attachment Styles 77
11 Relationship Boundaries 80
     Your Personal Forgiveness Project 83

Part III: MANAGING STRESS

12 Managing Stress & Emotions... 88
13 Prayer 94
14 Health & Wellness.. 99
15 Communication.. 103

Part IV: WRAP-UP & TEACH BACK

16 Wrap-Up 112
     Stuff Management Project 113
17 Final Reflections 115
Notes 118

Introduction

Before I share how *Don't Just Give "Your Stuff" Away*, came to be, I would like to introduce myself.

Hello my name is Princess Love and ***I AM A SURVIVOR***… I have survived marriage, child bearing, divorce, rejection, single parenthood, employment terminations, business failure, rebellion, and loss of friendships, gossip, infidelity, heart-break, critically ill children, being adopted, and death of a parent, not being loved, not being appreciated, bankruptcy, auto accidents, abortion, depression, racial and religious discrimination, unavailable men, shattered dreams, inadequate health care, college, unemployment, food stamps, child support battles, iniquity, welfare, poor health reports, graduate school, repossessions, foreclosure, deceptions, bad hair days, and poor decisions. By the Grace of God I made it through all of these challenging life events by walking in great expectation with Love. Like Oprah, I have moved on, to the next chapter in my life and I am determined to make it better than any of my past seasons.

Don't Just Give "Your Stuff" Away, began as a journal entry when I decided to document new scriptural rules for dating and relationships. Being discontented with my own relationship dilemmas, I re-read the story of Esther and spent some time with the Lord's commandments. Feeling inspired, I decided to create a few commandments of my own. The original list was very long as I continued to write orders against conditions that are contrary to healthy romantic relationships and friendships. During this process, I spoke with my aunt Elsie and asked if she wanted to hear what I was working on. When I shared my new dating commandments, she became so excited she immediately declared the list should become a book. Well, I uh um agreed with her, but I was really thinking what? You see a book in this, really? Regardless of what I was thinking and even if I did not completely agree with what she saw and what she said, the seeds of the book's concept were planted. In the following weeks I re-examined the list and began to add structure and order by separating the entries into categories based on particular themes. After the final lists were formed, the stories began to pour out of my experiences and the experiences of many friends. I began to see the book of healing stories, you are now holding.

I feel so blessed to answer the call to share the messages contained within this book with you. The core message is that each of us is in control of "our stuff;" and, we have the power to choose the types of relationships and lives, we would like to have. We are accountable for our thoughts, words, and deeds and we should take every measure to make them count for the good of everyone in our lives. Prepare to join me and many others on an amazing journey which is sure to initiate the healing of your heart and your life. Please open your hearts for a blessing from my heart to yours. All aboard! Toot, Toot!

As you board this ride with me, think about the words of Ms. Sojourner Truth in December of 1851. It was an address to the Women's Convention in Akron, Ohio, *"...he says women can't have as much rights as men, 'cause Christ wasn't a woman! Where did your Christ come from? Where did your Christ come from? From God and a woman! Man had nothing to do with Him... Ain't I a woman? ...If the first woman God ever made was strong enough to turn the world upside down all alone, these women together ought to be able to turn it back, and get it right side up again!..."*[1]

PART I

What Is "Your Stuff"?

My experience as a graduate counseling student was incredibly enlightening in many ways. The greatest truths I learned were focused on relationships and life lessons, which can easily be shared through personal stories. There seems to be a direct connection between the ears and the heart. An amazing thing happens when people listen and absorb the common pains and pleasures of others' personal journeys and testimonies. They are often validated and begin to heal from emotional injuries and painful memories, just by listening to other people's stories. For when a story speaks to us, it prompts us to monitor our vital signs and find the agreement or discord between our hearts, minds, and bodies. Stories with messages appearing to be personally designed for us often serve as triggers or alarms to help us get out of the messes we have gotten ourselves into. If a story speaks to us on multiple levels, it might prevent us from getting into trouble, in the first place.

I have decided to share a few of my stories and the stories gracious friends have given me permission to share as well. Most of these events happened many, many years ago but remain engaging and relevant. In order to protect my children and their privacy, the experiences I have shared do not include their fathers. For the record, I have one ex-husband and one "baby daddy," in that order. The baby daddy remark is shared in humor as he happens to be an excellent father. My children were never used to leverage or manipulate any of my relationship conflicts or outcomes. I hope our stories will help you identify the warning signs of unhealthy unions and gauge the conditions of your relationships. The purpose of this book is to provide a voice to start the conversations that will help women navigate through a better process of choosing and creating healthier and more fulfilling relationships. I am writing to girls and ladies of all ages, the young and the refined, and their mentors and protectors. My most passionate appeal goes out to the single and rebounding ladies everywhere.

Please note, I have changed names and limited other disclosing information about the people in our stories; it is more important that you see or feel what we learned than it is to be able to identify the participants. My goal is to use these stories and experiences to help you begin to consider what you need in order to manage your stuff.

Stuff Defined

When I first shared, with a few of my friends, the concept of not just giving your stuff away, we all smiled and giggled, just as you probably did when you first read the title. They all immediately thought of what author and producer Mr. Steve Harvey so affectionately defines as the "cookie" in his book *Act Like a Lady, Think Like a Man*.[1] The idea of the cookie is more of a complex energy system or a force of nature than a mere geographic hot spot. If you have not read the book, the cookie is the sweet spot located south of your belly button and covered by your bikini. Got it?

Before we proceed, let us take a moment to define "your stuff" to ensure a collaborative understanding, as we explore new ideals and the building blocks for authentic relationships. Your stuff is so much more than your cookie and you are much more than a cookie jar. Now, don't get me wrong, Mr. Harvey is 100% correct. The power of the cookie is paramount; however, it is not everything.

For the sake of this book, *"Your Stuff"* is defined as your Heart, Mind, Money, Body, Time, and Joy. Think of these as items of investments or currency you control in life and in particularly, within the realm of relationships. You have the power to negotiate and exchange these items to get what you need and to meet the needs of others. I do not know anyone who would consciously walk up to a complete stranger and hand over their life's savings. However, this is exactly what we do when we fail to manage our assets or "our stuff" and jump into new relationships without researching the partners of whose hands we place our investments. Your "heart stuff" includes your emotional condition and spiritual wellbeing. Your spiritual wellbeing addresses the essence of who you are, your core. Your "mind stuff" refers to how you think and process information, your mental health, and various types of education. Your "money stuff" indicates your income and financial resources from all sources. Financial conditions often reveal your career decisions and are reflections of natural gifting and skills, or lack thereof. Your "body stuff" involves the conditions of your physical body, nutritional health, fitness level, and the health of your reproductive system i.e. the cookie system. Your "time stuff" is a mirror of how you use all of your other stuff: your heart, mind, money and body. Time is the one thing you can never get back once it has been used or spent. So, use it wisely. Your "joy" refers to your perseverance in life. It indicates how you perceive events and reframe memories to work for you instead of against you. Joy is not about fleeting moments of happiness or excitement. When you have real joy, instead of looking for it you bring it with you. Joy allows you to laugh when others might cry, and it is accompanied by knowing who you are and knowing you have great purpose. Without joy, the greatest achievements and accumulations of wealth and prestige are void of pleasure and true value. Joyless living causes once treasured and honored accomplishments and relationships to feel meaningless and even tasteless.

It is my desire to enable and encourage you to make better decisions, so you may avoid the pitfalls that can cause women to actively participate in helping other people walk off with their stuff. One of the original discussions about "stuff" began back in 1975 when Ntozake Shange produced a choreopoem/play titled, *For Colored Girls Who Have Considered Suicide When the Rainbow Is Enuf*². In the play, a character who identifies herself as Juanita, speaks directly to this very condition. She repeatedly declares, "*…someone almost walked off with all of her stuff.*"[3]

Let me say right up front **this is not a man-bashing project in any way**. I did receive feedback from one reviewer who said it felt like man-bashing to her. To anyone who might be inclined to this opinion, I apologize. This is not my intention. The stories I share are not about making men look bad or women look good or innocent. They are about shining the light on unhealthy relationships and identifying signs of caution, *for women*. I am not a man hater; I actually love and embrace all the wonderful good things that make a man a man. A real man of faith and integrity is not likely to be offended by what will be shared in this book. Far too often, women continue to suffer the ill effects of relationships gone wrong, when their men move on with their lives. What I have written is the truth and sometimes the truth does hurt. Pain of truth is a sign some type of solution or treatment needs to be administered. I just want to start the healing process for as many women as I possibly can.

With the lists that follow in the next chapters, you should begin to develop a better understanding of the results created by negative or inappropriate behavior and unhealthy relationships. The stories provide pictures of real-life scenarios that may help you develop better practices which will improve your judgment, when it comes to understanding your own needs and discerning good character ingredients. The lists and stories will help you identify and avoid symptoms and circumstances that lead to unhealthy relationships. Some men could easily apply the same lists and standards to women. Nonetheless, I am speaking to women first because this is what my experience and gender dictate. However, I would also like to appeal to good men who truly care for the female relatives in their lives. Ladies, if there are brothers or sons in your lives, who are parents of young adult daughters, you should definitely recommend this book to them. Even though my language speaks directly to women, this project may also be a resource for dads and brothers. You dads and brothers who have accepted the invitation, this book can be used as a tool to help you articulate your concerns and cautions about specific types of characters you would like your daughters and sisters to avoid. Demanding orders like, "You better just stay away from that boy!" and "That jerk is bad news!" are not quite the effective declarations you would like them to be.

In addition to lists of characters and situations to avoid, we will explore boundaries, attachment styles, forms of relationship abuse, emotional and stress management, prayer, communication challenges and recommended wellness practices. All of these topics are directly connected to your stuff. If you have negative memories of how you handled your stuff in the past, make a choice not to live in those memories. Memories of the past should only be used to show us whom or what to avoid or embrace in the future. You must give up all hope of ever changing your past; your memories can never change your past and your memories can never fill your future, but you can.

The condition of giving our stuff away is so prevalent in today's society, because most of us have not defined boundaries and areas of personal ownership and responsibility with ourselves or within relationships. People take so many unspoken liberties with one another healthy boundaries are uncommon. The unfortunate experience of having poor boundaries and unhealthy relationships does not change the fact that we are designed for relationships. Our primary purpose for existence is to function and develop within the context of many relationships[4] and we all have an innate need to connect with others. The manner in which you manage your stuff has a direct correlation to the quality and satisfaction of all the relationships in your life. According to an article presented by Harvard Health Publications, relationships or social connections provide health benefits as compelling as exercise, a healthy diet, and adequate rest.[5] Unpleasant and antagonistic interactions with friends and family are associated with poor health.[6] A recent study of more than 300,000 people revealed the absence of strong relationships and important social ties is linked with depression and cognitive decline in older individuals, in addition to an increased risk of premature death.[7]

Relationships matter more than anything.

Through relationships we learn what is required for all stages of life, from the most basic functions of feeding ourselves and learning to tie our shoes, to the less basic activities such as playing sports and obtaining a driver's permit. We learn social and study skills, world concepts, and dating rituals through relationships. Everything you do or know has been taught, given, or modeled by someone you had some form of relationship with. Because of this, everything we do affects the people in our lives. Aside from the parent-child connection, the most significant human relationships are the relationships between men and women and husbands and wives. All relationships involve an exchange of stuff. When men and women struggle with difficulties in communicating and relating to one another, this exchange becomes unbalanced and the resulting pain and conflict affects all areas of their functioning, including other relationships.

It is imperative that we find a way to stop this madness. Stop giving our stuff away to unworthy suitors, so-called friends, and the causes that do not and cannot return the awesome love we have to share. Women are expected to be nurturing and giving helpers, made for service. I am here to tell you, it is possible to be a great lover, friend, and companion without giving all your stuff away.[8]

It's All About The Heart

Earlier when I defined "your stuff" I listed the heart first because it is one of the most important parts of your stuff. It is the seat of all emotions, positive and negative. From the heart flow all of the issues of our lives.[9] The heart reflects more than just what you feel, as it reveals what you believe about yourself, others, and the world you live in. Your heart stores the thoughts and memories of the past, and fuels the actions necessary for the birth of new dreams. When your heart is hurt or broken, it has the potential to pump the sadness and pain of heart-ache into all of your other stuff. In order to harness and maintain joy, you must learn to guard your heart. This is why I list it first and why we are strongly cautioned by wisdom to guard our hearts.[10]

Many people go through life unaware of potential choices present in every moment. Stereotypical views of women paint us as being good with making decisions about home décor, menu selection and preparation, teaching, demonstrating compassionate living, managing household operations, healing the sick and more, while staying fashion worthy. Somehow, the process of this natural knowing, automatic selection, and sound judgment abilities are forgotten when testosterone enters the room. Every moment of life demands some form of choice.[11] There is always something that needs to be done or not. Choices are made intentionally and consciously or unwittingly by failing to take the appropriate action. Not actively making a choice is a choice by default. Choosing a life full of joy and freedom begins with what you think and say[12] about whom you are and the life you would like to live. If you are currently in a relationship that does not honor or value you as the beautiful amazing person you were created to be,[13] you will find out how to regain your power (even under less than perfect circumstances), through a process of reclaiming your self-value. ***Ultimately, the condition of just giving away your stuff is not about unloving men and selfish women. It is more about self-perceived value reflected in your relationships.***

Now, please get comfortable. The style and tone of this book is conversational. English teachers and scholars, I ask for your forgiveness. I will not play by the rules. I want you as girlfriend readers (and concerned brothers) to feel like you are sitting in your family room on the comfy sofa or around the kitchen table with a few of your most special and closest friends.

At this point, I would suggest you obtain a journal to make the most of our time together. Make sure you select one that reflects aspects of your personality, so you can continue the process of keeping the journal, beyond the exercises I invite you to complete. Journals allow you to examine the past and the present while preparing for the future. A journal is an independent resource for many self-help programs. Your journal will allow you to track and document your personal change process and highlight information you will learn about yourself. The book is divided into four sections. The first section is The Lists & Relationship Stories and it focuses on how to navigate better results. In romantic and intimate relationships, it is not so easy to carve out the different entities that make up "our stuff." Our hearts and minds often get jumbled together and we are not completely sure of what we are feeling or thinking. When this happens, we have already unconsciously added our time to the equation and the progression of investing or sharing "our stuff" continues. I do not breakdown the "stuff" within the stories, but I do believe you will be able to see the steps of surrender we make toward partners who do not return the love, consideration, loyalty, or commitment we have given. Section two covers Core Beliefs and Boundaries which determine how we interact in relationships. Section three is about the many options for Managing Stress and section four is the Wrap-up and it includes an invitation to participate in your Personal Stuff Management Project.

Whenever you see this symbol, take out your journal to answer the questions and participate in a few exercises. Let us begin.

The Lists

The lists in the following pages spell out and catalog the results of negative behavioral characteristics, of men and a few women you should steer clear of. Detailed explanations of these characters are not in this chapter. I thought it would be beneficial to go through the lists before you begin to read the stories or reflect on your own stories. You will be able to identify characteristics or situations that are not so redeeming.

I want you to become familiar with the lists. You might think most of the lists are common sense; but, if you watch the news or any random reality television show, you will discover good sense is not common. Some of the descriptions are quite humorous while others are heavy. Many of the undesirables are duplicated in multiple categories. The lists are long and yes, they rule out a great number of men folk and imposture friends; but, you have to choose the quality of the relationships you would like to have. You do not have to sacrifice your value for companionship. Will it be easy? No. But we all know we have more appreciation for things we have to work for.

Within relationship paradigms, human nature indicates that we are quite selfish beings; yet, further observations reveal we are constantly giving ourselves away. Some of us build walls and barricades to keep others from entering our physically and emotionally sacred spaces and places, while simultaneously managing to empty our boudoirs of our most valued substances. We trade ourselves for unworthy tangibles, material concepts, and lies. We just give our stuff away. Some will hold onto a job, a purse, a car, an ill health report, or a piece of jewelry as if dear life depended upon it. We obsess over transient objects and ideals, in the midst of freely giving away our self-value and self-love, hearts, money, personal power, and our physical bodies. We cling to things that are without value or life and deny ourselves the true gift of life which resides within us.[1]

You do not have to settle for being almost compatible or a little happy. The signs of trouble are in big bold letters on the wall. They are not hidden and elusive as some ladies would like to pretend. There is a particular bill that is not discussed much. This bill is a bill of attention you have to pay in communication and relationships. You have to **pay attention** to what people are saying and not saying to you in every conversation or interaction. This one bill is worth every moment you spend on it. Paying attention will afford you information that may keep you from making poor decisions.

Although, I do not have personal stories to share about every undesirable on the lists, I am openly sharing some of the experiences I have had. We have all heard the saying, "Knowledge is power." I would like to clarify this statement by offering an updated version, "Knowledge is the beginning of power." You can know a lot of powerful information; but, if you don't do anything with that knowledge, it means nothing. Inactive knowledge is similar to the junk mail that fills your inbox or mail box. Power is created when you apply intelligent action to concrete knowledge. Prepare yourself to embrace both knowledge and power as we embark on this journey of stuff management, together.

1. THE UNAVAILABLE MEN LIST

Do NOT give YOUR STUFF to a man who is married to another woman.

Do NOT give YOUR STUFF to a man who is separated from his wife.

Do NOT give YOUR STUFF to a man in the process of getting a divorce.

Do NOT give YOUR STUFF to a man who is sleeping in a separate room in the house with his wife, while waiting for the divorce to be finalized.

Do NOT give YOUR STUFF to a man who is newly divorced.

Do NOT give YOUR STUFF to a man who is living with other women.

Do NOT give YOUR STUFF to a man still living with a woman he has broken up with.

Do NOT give YOUR STUFF to a man living with a female roommate.

Do NOT give YOUR STUFF to a man who wants to date other women while dating you.

Do NOT give YOUR STUFF to a man living with his baby's mama.

Do NOT give YOUR STUFF to a man who does not love you.

Do NOT give Your Stuff to a man you do not love.

Do NOT give YOUR STUFF to a man afraid of commitment or marriage.

Do NOT give YOUR STUFF to a man who says he needs to be alone.

Do NOT give YOUR STUFF to a man who says he never wants to marry.

Do NOT give YOUR STUFF to a man who is just not that into you.

Do NOT give YOUR STUFF to a man who won't introduce you to his friends or family.

Do NOT give YOUR STUFF to a man you will not introduce to your friends or family.

Do NOT give YOUR STUFF to a man who only visits during late hours.

Do NOT give YOUR STUFF to a man who never takes you out in public.

2. THE NON-FAMILY MEN LIST

Do NOT give YOUR STUFF to a man who does not like his mother.

Do NOT give YOUR STUFF to a man who does not like children.

Do NOT give YOUR STUFF to a man who supports abortion as a birth control option.

Do NOT give YOUR STUFF to a man who speaks negatively of his sisters.

Do NOT give YOUR STUFF to a man who does not love his family.

Do NOT give YOUR STUFF to a man who will not introduce his family.

Do NOT give YOUR STUFF to a man who does not have any friends.

Do NOT give YOUR STUFF to a man who will not discipline his children.

Do NOT give YOUR STUFF to a man who is not willing to spend quality time with his children.

Do NOT give YOUR STUFF to a man who does not fulfill his child support obligations.

Do NOT give YOUR STUFF to a man who is not compassionate.

Do NOT give YOUR STUFF to a man who is not serving the God you serve.

Do NOT give YOUR STUFF to a man who has no religion.

Do NOT give YOUR STUFF to a selfish man.

3. THE MAN-CHILD MEN LIST

Do NOT give YOUR STUFF to a man who is a boy.

Do NOT give YOUR STUFF to a man who cannot pay his own way.

Do NOT give YOUR STUFF to a man who does not want to work.

Do NOT give YOUR STUFF to a man who wants you to take care of him.

Do NOT give YOUR STUFF to a man whose mother takes care of him.

Do NOT give YOUR STUFF to a man who does not have any dreams or ambitions.

Do NOT give YOUR STUFF to a man who prefers spending time with his friends.

Do NOT give YOUR STUFF to a man who abuses his personal property.

Do NOT give YOUR STUFF to a man who does not fulfill his child support obligations.

Do NOT give YOUR STUFF to a man who cannot provide for your needs.

Do NOT give YOUR STUFF to a man who does not have good hygiene.

Do NOT give YOUR STUFF to a man who is financially irresponsible.

Do NOT give YOUR STUFF to a man who chases get rich schemes.

Do NOT give YOUR STUFF to a selfish man.

4. THE OFF LIMITS MEN LIST

Do NOT give YOUR STUFF to your Landlord.

Do NOT give YOUR STUFF to your Pastor.

Do NOT give YOUR STUFF to your Doctor.

Do NOT give YOUR STUFF to your Teacher or Professor.

Do NOT give YOUR STUFF to your child's Teacher or Coach.

Do NOT give YOUR STUFF to your neighbor's man.

Do NOT give YOUR STUFF to your boss at work.

Do NOT give YOUR STUFF to a co-worker in your immediate department.

5. THE NOT EVER MEN LIST

Do NOT give YOUR STUFF to your friend's man, ever.

Do NOT give YOUR STUFF to your sister's man, ever.

Do NOT give YOUR STUFF to your brother's man, ever.

Do NOT give YOUR STUFF to your cousin's man, ever.

Do NOT give YOUR STUFF to your mother's man ever.

Do NOT give YOUR STUFF to your Father, or Uncle, or Brother, or Cousin, ever.

Do NOT give YOUR STUFF to your Grandfather, Grandmother, or any step-parent or relative, ever.

Do NOT give YOUR STUFF to your children's friends, ever.

Do NOT give YOUR STUFF to a man on the Down-Low, ever.

6. THE DANGEROUS MEN LIST

Do NOT give YOUR STUFF to an angry man.

Do NOT give YOUR STUFF to a jealous or possessive man.

Do NOT give YOUR STUFF to a man who wants to control you.

Do NOT give YOUR STUFF to a man who stops you from spending time with family.

Do NOT give YOUR STUFF to a man who stops you from going to church or growing in your spirituality.

THE LISTS 13

Do NOT give YOUR STUFF to a man who behaves inappropriately in front of children or is attracted to children.

Do NOT give YOUR STUFF to a racist man.

Do NOT give YOUR STUFF to a man who is dishonest.

Do NOT give YOUR STUFF to a man who is violent.

DO NOT give YOUR STUFF to a man who hits you or curses you.

Do NOT give YOUR STUFF to who is always drunk.

Do NOT give YOUR STUFF to a man who has any addictions to drugs, sex, pornography, etc.

Do NOT give YOUR STUFF to a man who is untrusting of everyone.

Do NOT give YOUR STUFF to a confused or unstable man.

Do NOT give YOUR STUFF to a man who is involved in relationships with other men.

Do NOT give YOUR STUFF to a man who wants to be a woman.

Do NOT give YOUR STUFF to a woman who wants to be a man.

Do NOT give YOUR STUFF to a man who wants you to give your stuff to his friends.

Do NOT give YOUR STUFF to a man who does not respect women.

Do NOT give YOUR STUFF to a man who does not respect authority.

Do NOT give YOUR STUFF to a man for money.

Do NOT give YOUR STUFF to a man who makes you feel bad about your stuff.

Do NOT give YOUR STUFF to a man who is unwilling to meet your emotional needs

7. THE TOXIC FRIENDSHIP LIST

Do NOT give YOUR STUFF to a "friend" who is selfish.

Do NOT give YOUR STUFF to a "friend" who is jealous of you.

Do NOT give YOUR STUFF to a "friend" who lies to you.

Do NOT give YOUR STUFF to a "friend" who tells your secrets.

Do NOT give YOUR STUFF to a "friend" who makes advances on your boyfriend or husband.

Do NOT give YOUR STUFF to a "friend" who has slept with your boyfriend or husband.

Do NOT give YOUR STUFF to a "friend" who will not look out for you.

Do NOT give YOUR STUFF to a "friend" who flirts with you father.

Do NOT give YOUR STUFF to a "friend" who interferes with any of your other relationships.

Do NOT give YOUR STUFF to a "friend" who behaves inappropriately with your children

Do NOT give YOUR STUFF to a "friend" who borrows your clothes and returns them soiled or torn without compensation or apology.

Do NOT give YOUR STUFF to a "friend" who always wants you to pay for events you share.

Do NOT give YOUR STUFF to a "friend" who clearly is a gossip and untrustworthy.

Do NOT give YOUR STUFF to a "friend" who encourages you to behave inappropriately or to participate in illicit activities.

Do NOT give YOUR STUFF to a "friend" you cannot trust.

Unavailable Men

Unavailable men, outnumber all other men on the lists by far. As a descriptive term, unavailable (**un·a·vail·a·ble**) is commonly defined as: not available or inaccessible.[1] Other definitions include: missing; lacking; deficient; short; without; too little too late; inadequate; incomplete; insufficient; non-existent; vacant; absent; sketchy; and unsatisfactory. You get the picture. Descriptions that directly apply to the current topic are: preoccupied; busy; **engaged**; **involved**; **committed**; unattainable; unreachable; **inappropriate**; and **married**. Notice the words in bold? Married, engaged, involved, and committed all translate as **Unavailable**. Entering into a relationship with a man who is already in a relationship is never appropriate, acceptable, or smart. Unavailable men should be completely avoided. If you want a relationship that begins with honesty, you will need to lace up your tennis shoes and run from the men on this list

Unavailable men are unavailable regardless of what they tell you, how good they look, how smart they are, or how much money they make. One thing the men on this list can guarantee you is heartache. We do not have to share men. Ladies we must remember, men cannot step out on their commitments, if they do not have willing participants. They can only do to you what you allow them to do. If it helps, put yourself in the other woman's shoes. Would you want another woman sneaking around with your man or husband? I did not think so. Let us examine a little reality here. One real woman is more than enough for one real man. If a man thinks he needs more than one woman at a time, he is deceiving himself. He is only giving pieces of himself away to each of them, and he is suffering from secret inadequacies and a wounded past.

Now, there are men who only want to be with their wives. Unfortunately, these good men are not having their needs met, at home. Ladies, please take care of your men and keep them off the streets. It is safer for him, you, and your families in the long run. Imagine attending your favorite upscale restaurant requiring reservations and a dress code. You dressed up for the occasion and enjoyed a wonderful seven course meal. When you leave the restaurant, you run into an acquaintance, who invites you to get a bite to eat. Would you be interested or tempted to join him or her? No. Likewise, if you are meeting your man's needs both physically & emotionally, keeping him satisfied and full, he will not be tempted to dine without you. No matter how appetizing the other meal may appear, if he has committed to you and is a man of integrity, he will know and value his original cuisine. However,… a hungry puppy will eat from any hand willing to feed it. In *Act Like a Lady, Think Like A Man*, Mr. Harvey says men are more like dogs and will be loyal if you treat them right.[2]

Take your time with this list of unavailable men. As I said earlier, much of it may be common sense to you, but it may not be to your sister or sister-friend who has been deceived and lied to. Many times, these unavailable men do not reveal their current commitments, until it is obvious you have developed deep feelings for them.

My wise uncle Calvin told me, "If a man is willing lie to you, you should not be flattered. He is lying to protect himself and really does not care about you."[3] If we rule them out in the beginning, we will not have to deal with them when they spontaneously mutate into the liars and cheaters warranting a completely new list. Skip the drama and just say No! I also caution you not to deceive yourselves. Men rarely leave their wives for the other woman. You will not be able to change him or win him over. As a matter of fact, you have already given him much of your power if your current status is the other woman. Once you start giving your stuff away, it becomes increasingly difficult to stop.

If he cheats on her what makes you think he will not cheat on you? It does not matter how good you look or how good you are in bed. His cheating has nothing to do with you. It is best to just stay away. He should not have your stuff and his baby's mama's stuff too. He should not have your stuff on the weekends and his wife's stuff during the week. If he tells you he is no longer sleeping with her, he is lying. If you are not willing to kiss his baby's mama, his girlfriend, or his wife, you should not be kissing him. In doing so, you enter into her world, her business, and her health inventory. You are probably kissing parts of her you would rather not think about. Whatever she has contracted on her own or through him and his affairs, you can have it too. Is this something you would willingly sign up for?

Couples in the process of divorce can cancel the proceeding at any time before it is finalized. Even if a couple is still living together and claims they have ended the relationship, you must recognize they are often still emotionally and physically involved. You should not enter into a relationship with a man who has not applied the proper closure and distance to his past relationships. I say past relationships because he could still be involved with a woman who is not his current ex-woman or girlfriend. If they are actually married and have children, the affair will damage and wound all families involved, even if the affair has not been consciously revealed. I knew a woman who had legally separated from her husband. They realized the value of what they truly had and decided to reconcile. He came back home, only this time with a baby from another woman. My friend was a really great person with a kind loving heart and she accepted her man and his child. The difficult part was dealing with the baby mama drama and child support issues that placed demands on her purse too. Since they were married, a judge concluded his income included hers.

Do not respond to the friendship card often played by the unavailable man. A married man or committed man does not need any new single female friends, no exceptions. Becoming friends is an undercover way of creating and "alternate" door to something new and exploring possibilities of you giving your stuff to him at a later date.

Men know as women, we thrive on communication, support, making connections and building relationships. We possess natural emotional responses. Do not accept gifts from a committed man or allow him to do stuff for you around the house, for your car, or even your children. It is a sly way for him to enter your heart without asking permission. He has identified the back door access and will avoid the proper protocol to get what he wants, your stuff. Oh yes, and when he says he has never done this before, or you are the only one who has made him feel this way, do not believe him. Also, do not go for the claim of an open relationship or that his single female roommate is cool. This means she is a friend with benefits. How convenient is it that she lives with him?

I am sure you have heard the analogies about the cow and the milk. Is it not terrible that women are compared to cows? Anyway, the question is why would a man buy a cow while he is getting all its good milk for free? There are several types of gentlemen who tip toe around this scenario to avoid commitment. Now, there are men who do not want to buy the cow, nor do they want to lease it with the option to buy later. This type of man just wants the retail benefits of receiving the premium harvest creamy milk without any responsibility of caring for or even grooming the cow. This man is just not that into you. He is using you and he will be your prime booty call initiator. You are worth so much more; do not waste any of your time with him. Instead, save all of your stuff for a worthy suitor. You do not want to be tangled up with the wrong guy when the right one comes along. Don't take that chance.

Unfortunately, you may have seen your sister, mother or aunt become involved with Unavailable men. You do not have to. These sister-friends may not have been taught this was not appropriate or maybe they did not believe they had other options. Some of our sisters and friends have been abused by men and life in general. These women have not learned how to value themselves enough to make the better choice. You have the power to choose what is good and acceptable.[4] Most women are not dating without a purpose. We are all looking for a special someone to share our lives with. We want a witness to the wonderful gift of life. For the greatest life satisfaction, it is important to know your rights and not settle or compromise the standards which will establish the foundation of a healthy and rewarding relationship.

For those of you, who have grown accustomed to blaming the devil on all the bad things that happen to you, Just Stop It! You are giving him way too much credit and power. Most of the time, we become his entertainment. We do his work for him, through poor decisions, self-destructive habitual patterns, and spiritual drought. You may encounter overwhelming temptations; however, the end result reflects your choice. Again I repeat, every moment offers a choice. You either choose consciously and proactively or unconsciously by lying dormant and not using the beautiful mind and heart you were born with. If you chose to become sexually active before achieving true commitment or marriage, clearly the choice is yours. We do not fall in or out of love, and no one accidentally falls into sex. Let us not kid ourselves. Some type of planning and arrangements have to be made before two people come together to have sex. Sex is a lot of things but it is never an accident.

You determine what standards you choose to live by. And you will be known by those standards. You decide what is acceptable for your stuff, no one else can do that for you. While you are in the moment of each choice of your life, you must also know a divine plan has been created, with you in mind. Just be honest with yourself because this is another area of great self-deception. Do not deceive yourselves about oral sex. Keep it real ladies. Oral sex is sex as the name implies. You are not just friends or practicing abstinence or celibacy if you are having oral sex. You are no longer in the getting to know you as a friend stage if you are kissing down there. You are in fact sexually active. He is still getting your stuff and is more likely to get more of it later; since, it is obvious you are already quite comfortable with him.

There are three things you need to think about and do before you prepare or chose to share any of your stuff.

Three Things

1. You need to get to know yourself and take steps to add closure to any unfinished business and heal old wounds. Get rid of your excess baggage.
2. You need to establish some rules about your stuff and determine what is important to you.
3. You need to know what you want in a man and in a relationship, what you can live with and what you cannot live without. After this preliminary work you need to position yourself to observe him in different scenarios and verify who your prospective man presents himself to be.

Next, start with The Observation/Information Gathering Check List

THE OBSERVATION/INFORMATION CHECK LIST & THE LOAV METHOD

Listen: Get to know him by intentionally listening to what he says and does not say in conversations. Eye contact is important. Most people are uncomfortable with direct eye contact when they are being less than honest. If they attempt to do so, there are some signs that will give them away. Avoid overt deliberate sexual flirtations while you are getting to know him. Once the sexual banter and touching begins, the getting to know stage often ends abruptly. This is how the "sleeping with the enemy" condition begins. Sleeping with the enemy begins with sleeping with a stranger.

Observe: Check out his body language when he interacts with you and others. Observe him in as many different scenarios as possible: interacting with his friends, family members, children, mother, siblings, church members, exes, and co-workers whenever possible. Observe his behavior and interaction while on dates. How does he behave on dates? Is he considerate and polite? Is he patient with you and people who serve him? Is he attentive?

Ask the questions: Do not be afraid to ask questions. You will be surprised by how much information you receive just by asking the right questions. Take note if he has difficulty answering basic questions. If he is serious he should also have some questions for you.

Verify: Verify the information he has given you about his employment, residence, marital status, number of children, education, living arrangements, hobbies, etc. Please don't be shy about this step. You do not have to hire a private detective. We live in the age of advance technology and information. Facebook and LinkedIn are just a few of easy non-invasive places to start your research and verification.

Stress Management, Family Life & Spiritual Health

Primary areas you need to study about your prospective partner include Stress Management, Family Life, and Spiritual Health. This trio will provide the information you need to determine how compatible you are and how you will work through challenges, disappointments, and this thing called life. It is just a start. You can begin with these observations and questions and create a few of your own in each section.

The questions are to get you thinking and to help you shape and analyze the information you gather. The answers will come from your observations and questions. Please complete your homework and research. Due diligence is mandatory.

Consumer guides and other resource engines are flooded with inquiries from people preparing to make an appliance purchase, select a vacation spot, or view feedback on a local restaurant. Your stuff being your life and wholeness is more meaningful than these things which are often regarded with greater importance. In the beginning of relationships people are normally on their best behavior. This is the very reason you need to take your time. There are some great board games that will also provide a glimpse of the inner working, thought patterns, and habits of most people. A few fun games include Taboo, Apples to Apples, Clue, and of course the game of Life.

Stress Management: Find out how he deals with stress and challenging situations. Does he have a temper? Has he ever hit a woman? Does he drink to forget? Does he work out? What does he do for fun? Has he ever used drugs? Does he have any health challenges? Is he taking specific medications? What does vacation mean to him? It is not likely you will get all of these answers up front. It will take time, trust building, and the right timing. You should not be in a hurry.

Family Life: What was his home like? You want to know what kind of family structure he had and who were his role models? What is his concept of women's roles? If his role models were disrespectful to women, he will find it difficult to behave differently. What are his beliefs on child rearing? Does he get along with his siblings? Does he enjoy family gatherings? Does he have happy childhood memories? How much time does he spend with his family? Does he think his parents did a good job with him? Was he loved and cherished as a child? Were his physical and emotional needs met? Does he want children?

Spiritual Health: What are his spiritual beliefs? Has he defined spiritual beliefs independent of his family's spiritual history or ancestry? Ask about his spiritual life and activities. Is he connected to a church family, a synagogue, a temple, or does he consider himself an independent? Does he pray or meditate? What is his worldview? Ask the questions and you will get answers.

ASK THE QUESTIONS!

Now let's take a closer look at the Unavailable Man list.

THE UNAVAILABLE MEN LIST

Do NOT give YOUR STUFF to a man who is married to another woman.
Do NOT give YOUR STUFF to a man who is separated from his wife.
Do NOT give YOUR STUFF to a man in the process of getting a divorce.
Do NOT give YOUR STUFF to a man who is sleeping in a separate room in the house with his wife, while waiting for the divorce to be finalized.
Do NOT give YOUR STUFF to a man who is newly divorced.
Do NOT give YOUR STUFF to a man who is living with other women.
Do NOT give YOUR STUFF to a man still living with a woman he has broken up with.
Do NOT give YOUR STUFF to a man living with a female roommate.
Do NOT give YOUR STUFF to a man who wants to date other women while dating you.
Do NOT give YOUR STUFF to a man living with his baby's mama.
Do NOT give YOUR STUFF to a man who does not love you.
Do NOT give Your Stuff to a man you do not love.
Do NOT give YOUR STUFF to a man afraid of commitment or marriage.
Do NOT give YOUR STUFF to a man who says he needs to be alone.
Do NOT give YOUR STUFF to a man who says he never wants to marry.
Do NOT give YOUR STUFF to a man who is just not that into you.
Do NOT give YOUR STUFF to a man who won't introduce you to his friends or family.
Do NOT give YOUR STUFF to a man you will not introduce to your friends or family.
Do NOT give YOUR STUFF to a man who gives out his cell number.
Do NOT give YOUR STUFF to a man who only visits during late hours.
Do NOT give YOUR STUFF to a man who never takes you out in public.

HOW I KNOW

Parker

I believe we unconsciously know unavailable men are not options. Somehow this "knowing" we should avoid unavailable men gets lost in the hype of Hollywood, other media and social deceptions, poor relationship modeling, and rogue hormones. Many years ago, I made a decision I would consciously avoid unavailable men. Unfortunately, I still managed to fall prey to their tactics and games.

I was a Certified Mixologist (a fancy name for a Bartender) for a local night club in Washington, DC. I wasn't a drinker; so, the alcohol was not a problem. I was propositioned regularly and this was not a problem either. Eventually, I was caught up. There was this gentleman who worked for a law enforcement agency in the city, Parker. Parker was twice my age. I know it doesn't sound right but he took great care of himself. He worked out regularly and still held his own, in games of football with his son and his son's friends, who were also around my age. Parker was more subtle in his approach of pursuing me; he did not proposition me directly like many of his peers and others who frequented the club. He was the nice gentleman who talked about his sons, his wife, and his family. I thought he was safe because he did not pursue me. At this time, I was also not available.

Time passed and eventually I ended my employment at the club. I was out of touch with the employees and customers and Parker and I ran into each other. Now, I was a year older and my previous relationship had also ended. I felt empowered with a new sense of freedom.

If you know anything about DC, you know you do not need a car. Actually, in many instances, owning a car could be more of a burden than a benefit; and I did not have one. So, Parker asked me out for lunch and I didn't think anything of it. He was safe remember; when I first met him, he did not pursue me or signal in any way that he was out to get me or any of "my stuff." One lunch date lead to another. He began to give me rides around town and he would even offer to pick up a few extras for my apartment. At this point, we were minding our manners; but, I had come to care for him differently. Just as the summer approached, he told me his wife was leaving him and taking his sons with her. She no longer wanted to be married to him. His wife's hometown was across the country. She would be far from him and she was taking his sons. I hurt for him. Needless to say, our relationship changed and I felt the need to console and care for him. Somehow, he had already accessed my heart and I began giving him more of my thoughts, my time, and eventually my other stuff.

The summer was a blast. We had crab feasts at the Awakening, we toured fun areas of the city, we dined, and he got a lot of my stuff. We became regulars at a hotel in the city and he even took me to his home. He did allow me to see him at work…after hours.

Just as this wonderful summer began to close, Parker came to me and told me his wife and sons had returned home. He said she decided it would be better for his children to go to school there with him. After his children were settled for the school year, his wife would return to her mother's home. I believed it. Later he came back and told me she has changed her mind and had decided to stay. What was this supposed to mean? I thought it was over between them. Why would she do this? I was floored. What do you do with that? He was still trying to make me think it really was over between them.

I was thankful I had an opportunity to speak with one of our mutual friends who was willing to tell me the real truth. Parker's wife never left him. She did not want out of the marriage; she was away on a work related summer project which just happened to be in her hometown. Because of this, she was able to stay with her mother and spend time with her family. This enabled her to take their boys along for the trip. His wife was a very beautiful woman; in fact, she was so beautiful she was often mistaken for a model. No, they were not having any marital complications. Can you imagine that! *It was all a lie!* Call me stupid if you want to but this kind of deception happens more often than you think.

The funny thing is I was so hurt; I called my ex-boyfriend, Steven. I told him what happened; Parker keeps calling; but, I refuse to answer his calls. Parker left message after message; but, there was nothing he could say. I did not want to speak with him. Steven gave me excellent advice which comes from what I call 'man' knowledge. After all, he was a man and knew how men thought. He told me not to return the calls and that I had done the right thing. He told me if I had even one conversation with Parker, he would try to convince me of another preposterous story, try to find a way to get back with me, and getting more of my stuff. Steven told me Parker knew I cared for him and he would use this information against me to get what he wanted. I never spoke to him again.

I will not use it as an excuse; however, I did not grow up with any brothers or even male cousins to be able to learn from their activities or motivations. Ignorance is not bliss. Don't judge, just help. If you are a female who has had the advantage of this foreknowledge, please share it with your sisters who are naïve and clueless, as I was. When I think back, I can see how he watched me, studied me, and knew what would be needed to get my stuff. It was not by coincidence that we ran into each other. It was his plan.

WHAT I FAILED TO DO

First of all, I had not taken the first three self-care steps to prepare for any relationship.

1. ***Get to know yourself and take the steps to add closure to unfinished business and heal old wounds. Get rid of your excess baggage.***
   I had no business entering into a relationship with anyone at the time. I had unfinished business. I had not taken the time to reflect on what I learned from my last unsuccessful relationship. What worked for us and what didn't? Why was this special relationship being dissolved? Why did I no longer want to be with a man whom I once loved like crazy? For a season, I felt he was my soul mate. Steven had helped me see things about myself and the world, things I had not known before; and, now it was ending. This should have been a time of getting to know me. You would think, as an adult I would have learned how to make adult decisions. If I had worked on myself instead of looking for the next distraction or feel good, I would have made more mature decisions. I should have sought counsel. But, who seeks counsel when they know they are not behaving appropriately.

2. *Establish rules about Your Stuff and what's important to you.*
   I had not examined what was important to me. I may not have set out to become involved with a married man; but I had not established real boundaries. I had not decided what was important to me and how valuable my stuff really was. In this case, it wasn't about insecurity; it was ignorance.
3. *Know what you want in a man, what you can live with and what you cannot live without.*
   I was free but undefined. I did not know what I wanted or what I couldn't live without. This left me open to the wrong opportunity.

Let's look at the LOAV Method
Listen - Observe - Ask –Verify

Listen. We have two ears and one mouth for a reason. If we could learn to listen twice as much as we talked our lives would be so different. If I had listened with purpose and asked questions, I may have learned he was lying much earlier.

Observe. I did not observe him in different scenarios. Although I knew he was a man who fought for justice, I did not find out he abused his power until much later. I never met any of his family members and did not have an opportunity to observe his co-worker's reactions to meeting me. I never met any of these important people in Parker's life, and we did not have many discussions about them. I did visit his home but believed his wife had left him.

Ask Questions I did not ask the right questions or enough questions. We did not talk about what his parents were like or who his family models were. I did not learn about his spiritual condition as I was a lost child at the time, as well. If I asked more questions I might have realized he was bi-curious and experimented with a variety of sexual appetites. These are things a woman should want to know about a man she is involved with.

Verification. Verification needs to happen over time. Situations may be established on a short term basis which appear to be real, yet do not reflect the whole truth. I failed miserably in this area. The gentlemen he associated with at the night club often exhibited lower levels of character than he did. Even so, they had information I did not have. I could have contacted them, for a friendly chat. He did allow me to visit his office, but only after office hours. No one was there to see us. He would not have to introduce me or explain who I was. I did not know his wife would only be away for the summer. Stress Management was and issue for Parker. He drank more than I would have liked; and, I began to notice he used alcohol to relieve his stress. Playing football with the boys didn't quite do it for him. Eventually, it became apparent; my stuff became part of his stress management program.

I allowed this interaction to develop entirely too fast. Fast has its place; but, not in relationships. Please take your time to get to know a man BEFORE you make a decision to determine if he is worthy of receiving any of your stuff. Listen, Observe, Ask, and Verify who he presents himself to be especially when it comes to stress management issues, family functioning and spiritual health. Please ask the questions!

My Spiritual Development in Process

Let me pause here for a moment to set up a back drop of my own spiritual processing at this time in my life. I began my spiritual journey at the age of six. I pleaded with my mother to allow me to attend church with our neighbors who were members of a local Pentecostal congregation. I remember it being referred to as a Holiness Church. There was so much excitement I was drawn to it, the music, the dancing, and the passion for God. My family's denomination was Episcopal. At the age of 11 along with my sisters, I was christened.

As the years passed, my family seemed less interested in attending services so the church youth ministry began to provide transportation for me. My high school began with the eighth grade; and, this was the year a friend invited me to her church. Marjory attended an apostolic church which became the home to my new beginning. It provided very similar experiences I enjoyed many years before. I was baptized there when I was 13 years old. Unfortunately, my parents did not share my concerted spiritual interests. I explained my experience and what it all meant. I even took out my Bible and showed my father the books of John and Acts so he could get a clearer picture of my experience. I was baptized in the name of Jesus. I shared about going down in the water and how amazing I felt when I surfaced. My friends Marjory and Chris attended my baptism. Both commented about the indescribable beautiful glow surrounding me when I rose from the water. I could feel whatever it was that they saw.

Immediately following my baptism, I was taken into a quiet upper room where a woman prayed for and with me. During this prayer, I became aware of the gift of the Holy Spirit being deposited on the inside of me and the gift of speaking in tongues. A day I will never forget.

It was challenging to remain in the spiritual envelop without strong spiritual family supports. As time passed, I was caught up with all of the typical challenges teenagers faced in the 80s. Goals of purity, celibacy, and sanctification had great competition. Parents do not always teach their children how to make good choices or what or specific signs for situations they need to avoid or actually run away from. Orders to stay away from boys and not to be so "fast" are not compelling learning objectives. So much is left up to chance or the fear of parental wrath and we all know neither option is effective. When I went off to college, I still had some semblance of a relationship with God. Of course, I said my prayers regularly and talked to him on occasion but it was not the personal or truly intimate relationship I have since grown into.

In college, a friend introduced me to Tarot cards and Wicca. I met a gentleman on campus who had similar curiosities and we began to study and practice as Wiccans. We called ourselves "good witches." I was definitely off the original path; yet it was still part of the spiritual pursuit my Heavenly Father allowed. When Wicca no longer satisfied us we began to explore traditional African religions and were initiated as priest and priestess in the Akan and later into the Yoruba religions. Both of these faiths worshiped multiple deities, honored ancestors and guardian spirits and Jesus was not one of them. I still prayed to the God I knew in my heart, but I no longer wanted to acknowledge Jesus. Interestingly enough, some of these religions had worship practices not very different from Pentecostal, Apostolic, and Baptist worship services.

Through our initiations and rites of passage we learned, self-control, temperance, discernment, and self-preservation. We rose at dawn to pray, pour libations, and dance as a form of worship. We had a curfew, dietary restrictions, and had to abstain from sexual relations for three months. I learned a lot about myself during this time. My blessing is that I already knew Jesus. Even though I had walked away from him, he never left me and even though I experienced many fires and life storms I emerged intact and whole.

It was when our eyes were opened to the political strategies embedded into these religions, in the houses we were associated, we planned our departure. I left these homes of worship but I did not leave behind what I learned and I took the deities with me. I continued to worship them privately. I did not claim any part of Christianity, as I had learned how so many Christians used this faith to cause harm to others. When I met Parker, I was still a Yoruba initiate. I had a private alter containing the memorabilia and artifacts of the Orisha and guardian spirits I served. You are about to read about a man named Grayson. I carried my Orisha into my relationship with him also. My worldview was not Christian.

Grayson

Let me tell you about Grayson. I met Grayson a few years after I stopped seeing Parker. Grayson is the ultimate and the most dangerous unavailable man you are likely to encounter. What makes him dangerous? He is not dangerous because of violence; what makes him dangerous is his thorough knowledge of you. He is familiar and comfortable and you already love him. You know him and he knows you well. Grayson is your ex-boyfriend, ex-man, or ex-husband. When you have created real closure with an ex, it is natural to feel severe sadness as you mourn the loss of the relationship. If the process of mourning is complete you will be less inclined to return to an unhealthy or unhappy experience, which led to the break up in the first place. A second time around with unresolved issues has the potential to cause even greater damage to your self-concept. Ambiguous scenarios present themselves when you have unfinished business and the relationship did not reach an official status of closure. A lack of closure can cause complications and increased likelihood that you could return to the same dysfunction, because you when you still hold passion and love for each other. When intimate romantic relationships end, they really need to end. If your relationship cannot officially end, you need to be brutally honest with one another and research and dissect the truth about what's going on in the relationship and why. Unfortunately, married couples often complete divorce proceedings, before truly understanding why the relationship is ending.

Your ex knows what you like and what you don't like; he knows what your buttons are and how to push them. Romantic couples breakup for many reasons, sometimes it's about money, infidelity, and jealousy. Sometimes it's about a lack of communication or the inability to meet each other's emotional, physical, or intellectual needs. As a young person, I thought Tina Turner was crazy when she sang *"What's love got to do this it?"*[5] In my mind, love had everything to do with it. With love a couple can conquer any obstacle life throws in their path, right? This is not completely true. I have sense learned; love alone is not enough to sustain a healthy rewarding relationship. When you are considering a breakup and you know you still have strong feelings for the other person, collect yourself and the relationship to find out why you think you are ready for this union to end. You need to know for sure it has ended or you will not be able to truly move on. It may be helpful to seek a professional relationship counselor before you call it quits. Do not fool yourself and do not play games.

Without effective closure you will find yourself open, hopeful, and wishing to be reunited, when the pain and aggravation subsides. He may have moved on but you have not. He may have started a new relationship and still have a desire to be with you. He will tempt and test your boundaries. A man knows when you want to be with him, many will capitalize on this knowing.

If you are not careful, you may settle for becoming a type of friend you have never been to him before, friends with benefits. He could be moving forward in a new relationship and still make time to come around and visit you. What does this make you? It makes you the other woman. Please do not try to rationalize or justify your position. You have become his secret and the one he visits under the guise of shadow and darkness, not fully acknowledged in the position you would like to occupy in his heart or his life. If he truly cared for you, he would not allow this to happen, even if it meant denying his own desires. When you were together he may have been completely faithful to you. Note I say may; because if he can do this with another woman, who is to say he did not behave in this way when he was with you.

Grayson was able to seduce and reduce me into being the other woman. How was he able to do this? I still loved him and I let him. I had passion for him. I wanted to love him and made the choice to allow him in again. The irony is I ended our relationship, the first time around. When I ended the relationship I was not feeling the love I needed and thought we both had some growing to do. More than anything, I wanted him to realize I was the best choice for him. How could he not see all this beautiful, smart, talented woman right in front of his face? What was wrong with him? Well, it never happened and I had to realize he was just not that into me and it was not about me. Men are also entitled to their choices as well. He had made a different choice I would have to live with. Coming to terms with this was not easy but I committed myself to the healing process and retreated from interacting with him.

Meeting Grayson the First Time

So where did I meet him? We met in a local gym in DC. I can still remember the first moment I saw him. I experienced shivers and was smitten with him from that moment on. We had this amazing chemistry that would not go away and we were once so connected. After dating for a few months, we practically moved in together. He did not have to pack an overnight bag when he visited me; because so many of his things were already at my place and vice versa. We were inseparable for a season; it was the two of us against the world. There were not many things I would not be willing to do for him and he made me feel like he would do anything for me. There was a time when we shared our dreams and aspirations and communication was good. I felt continually intoxicated with his love, care, and passion for me. I can remember many nights pretending to put him on like a garment. I would pretend to unzip his back and motion as if I had stepped into him. I imagined what it felt like to be him. It felt strong, powerful, and rooted. Previous relationships and even my relationship with my father(s) never felt as secure as I felt with him. I finally felt like someone had my back and I did not have to do all the fighting. He made me feel like a woman (not just in bed) in ways I had not experienced before and I liked it!

Maintaining a position of personal power is greatly determined by whom or what you allow to enter your heart.

He did many things for me and looked after all of my needs. If I needed something he got it. If I wanted something he got it. So, naturally I was trying to give him all of my stuff at any moment possible. He had my heart and mind on lock-down and this gave him access to everything else. Maintaining a position of personal power is greatly determined by whom or what you allow to enter your heart. I attempted to indulge every fantasy he thought he had. I even watched inappropriate films with him and invited another woman into our bedroom. Please don't do this! I thought it was not be a big deal. Coming from a theater community I saw a lot of things and was told what grown folks do is their business. I was open to trying new things and curious about many other things. At the time, I was unaware of the travesties happening to women through the industry. As my naive invincible self, I had this motto to try everything at least once and if you like it try it again. I had no reason to be suspicious of infidelity; I handled my business and handled it well…so I thought.

A gentleman I dated briefly, before I met Grayson came into town and I let Grayson know. Grayson told me to, "Be careful to not get yourself or this guy hurt." This sounds threatening but Grayson was never physically aggressive with me. He was the King of my jungle and he was letting me know it. I remember smiling from ear to ear when he said this. I had not had a responsible King before. I could not imagine he would ever hurt me and I let it be known I was extremely happy at home. Memories include attending concerts, sharing dreams, dancing, and exploring all the city had to offer, together. I also enjoyed playing house and taking care of him. Trouble in paradise was not too far off. All this love, good loving, and good times did not keep something from his past from reaching up to where we were, and eventually robbing us of our future.

The following summer, I took a trip home to spend some time with my family. While I was away, I was unable to reach him for about three days. This was quite disturbing for me. We had never gone this long without communicating since our relationship began. This unaccounted for time represents the first planting of doubt and distrust into our relationship.

When I returned, Grayson gave me some lame excuse about hanging out with some friends. At the time I did not have any proof he was unfaithful and eventually let it go. For many, this would have ended the relationship. Why would I not let this go? (I'll answer this question a little later.) Looking back, I can now say this was the beginning of the end. It took a few years for the end to arrive; but the end started with this situation. After this event, I began to wonder what he was doing and where he was, when we were not together. I became suspicious of the young woman we invited in and entertained. I also became suspicious of his female co-workers. I had not done this before. If you knew me, you knew I was typically opinionated, strong minded, and self-confident; but, this made me suspicious and insecure. I did not wear it well. It was not part of my original make-up. Don't let people give you what doesn't belong to you. This newfound insecurity did not belong to me.

From this moment, our communication began to change. I no longer felt he was as open with me in ways he used to be. If I did something he didn't like he would not speak to me for a few days. He never hit me or called me names, and he was never violent with me in any way, but for me the silent treatment felt like a beat down. It seemed his usual communication style was not as open and engaging as he represented in the beginning. Like most people, he wanted things done his way. If I would not or could not complete a task the way he wanted, it was best not to do it at all.

Another incident arose and marked additional conflict in our compatibility. A close relative of mine came into town and dropped by one afternoon. Grayson was surprisingly rude and insensitive. I did not understand why the visit had to be so difficult. At the end of the evening, he revealed he behaved the way he did to see how I would respond. There is definitely something wrong with someone needing to test your relationship in this way. The next thing I knew he started working late, one of the number one lies a man uses when he is cheating or exploring other options is that he was "just working late." The rest is history.

WHAT I FAILED TO DO AGAIN!
Three Things
1. *Get to know yourself and take the steps to add closure to unfinished business and heal old wounds. Get rid of your excess baggage.*

   I was single and not in another relationship. I had not spoken with Parker and would not be tempted in anyway to reunite with him. It was completely over. I had a decent job, rented my own apartment and felt a renewed sense of freedom and independence. However, I had not taken measures to redefine who I wanted to be at this point in my life. As a side note I must also mention my spiritual state was not clearly defined. The spiritual system I practiced at the time was empowering in many ways; nonetheless, it did not instill the personal value and provision which is interjected when you can call on Jesus. In my times of crisis, I did in fact call on Jesus. These indigenous religions also supported practices allowing men to have multiple wives. Would this make cheating okay? Was I unconsciously open to being a sister-wife, because of this exposure? When was this idea or concept planted?

2. **Establish rules about Your Stuff and what's important to you.**
   From the beginning, we moved entirely too fast. I had not established rules or boundaries about relationships or sexual intimacy. A month passed before we had sex. This was during a time when people did not wait. He did not rush me into bed and I thought this was special. I now know it was not. A month is still too soon. Once I began to share my stuff with him, it was like my drug. It controlled me and my judgment went out the window. In my mind, he was a real man and I had not had a real man before. Basically, I lost power in the relationship after a mere four weeks because I gave up all my stuff too soon.

3. *Know what you want in a man, what you can live with and what you cannot live without.*
   I had no idea what I was headed into and had still not defined what I wanted or needed. He was a man who took care of me and I wanted to love him so much. In the beginning, he made me feel loved and cherished in a new way. Communication is so important to me and to any relationship for its strength and survival. I did not know what he wanted. For a season I know he wanted me but the season changed. We never regained the level of communication we had in the beginning.

Take out the the LOAV Method
LOAV: Stress Management - Family Life - Spiritual Health

Listen: We talked a little about sexual experiences but we also had conversations about many other things in the beginning. He claimed to be Christian and I did not. Yet, he was still interested in dating me. Did he believe he could convert me? I do not know; but, I was way out there then.

Observe: Before he moved to a new location, I never visited his home. I did travel out of town to visit one of his aunts who was ill at the time. He did invite me to visit him at his job during lunch time. I did not meet his children or ex for several months. His parents were much older and his father had recently passed.

Ask: I did not ask enough questions I did not collect enough information to allow me to make the decisions I made.

Verify: All of his general information seemed to be correct. What I did not find out until much later is, he was living with another woman when we met. He lived with her several months after we began dating and before he moved into his own place. Prior to this relationship, he had been divorced for almost two years and had two sons. He was a huge Redskins fan, enjoyed working out and, taking care of himself. Other positives were that he did not smoke and was not a heavy drinker.

Stress Management: He had an issue with bottling up his anger. I thought his stress management strategy encompassed his fitness goals and working out. I learned it was not always effective. He was a brooder and still angry about past childhood experiences. He could go days without speaking. For me, this was like a slow suffocation.

Family Life: I learned he did come from a loving family. Both of his parents had passed away before I met him. He was one of five, two boys and three girls. If he wanted anything, he had to work hard to get it. No one ever gave him anything and he did not see anything as easy. This tough upbringing caused him to think no one else should have it any easier than he did.

Spiritual Health: He went to church when he was younger and he reports his parents being very strict with a more traditional doctrine. He did not go to church anymore but he did believe in God. He did not have an observable active spiritual life.

Grayson Part II

Grayson and I ended the relationship and we attempted to move on with our separate lives. At a point of distress, I found myself back in a local church of the apostolic faith. It felt like home again. I begin to read the bible more and learn more about the real person of Jesus Christ. Once again, another friend, Greg invited me to church and I went. It was not long before I accepted a study challenge. I completed the study, joined the church, and began to prepare for my rededication. I turned from my old way of thinking and living and I was taken back into the fold and baptized again. This time I was more aware of the choice I made and what it truly meant.

A few years had passed and one of my girlfriends played match-maker and tried to fix me up with one of her friends. This did not work out. I quickly discovered the gentleman actually had feelings for her and by this time, I had new goals for my life and a new perspective of dating. I was not going backwards; I had learned some important lessons. My choices embraced my Lord in a new way. I felt like I had gotten out of jail and my bondage and burdens had been lifted. I helped my friend and the gentleman she tried to match me up with, begin an honest conversation and they became a couple. As the season changed, I met a few gentlemen and finally began dating a bit myself. I was begged by a dear friend to try eHarmony and I did. I even traveled to Richmond to meet one of the three prospects I met online and I was doing okay. The gentlemen I met were nice but none of them seem to have the special ingredients I was looking for. I liked them, but the connections were not deep enough. I was never sexual with any of them. I had a three date kiss rule and never seemed to make it to the third date. The only exception was my Richmond connection. We had emailed for a few months and talked on the phone another few months. But the kiss was the extent of our touching. I had gained a sense of control in this area and thought of sex differently. If you are wondering, he did think the night might turn out differently. Sex was completely off the table for me. I had become aware that I was never alone and the Spirit of God was always present. As a matter of fact, I had the revelation I had been aware of the Holy Spirit's presence since I was six. He was still there even when I walked away. Anyway, I generally do not do things I consciously do not want to do. If I wanted to, it would have been a different story. It turned out we were not quite the right match for each other. I am so grateful we did not "hook-up."

As it happened, I ran into Grayson on the bus one day and we updated our contact info. I was not in a relationship and he had just met someone but he said it was not "that serious." Over the phone we began to catch up. We talked a little about our relationship and what went wrong. It was obvious he was still hurt by my leaving but it was also obvious he missed me. I asked him if he wanted to get to know each other again and he agreed. I added the stipulation that we needed to leave the sex out. We already knew how those parts worked but if we were going to try again, I wanted to work on the friendship first. He agreed but then asked what we would do when the desire showed up? I said we could walk, pray, or do something to distract those thoughts or feelings. Again he agreed and we started spending non-sexual time together. This was fine until I began to rationalize my position and the circumstances of our relationship. I was encouraged by a friend who thought Grayson and I were meant to be together. She was already married and she recommended I should do whatever I needed to do to reclaim my relationship and him. She shared how she fought for her husband and it worked out for her. Hmm. I began to rationalize he would probably be my husband if I had not ended the relationship. It must be our fate because we have reconnected. Obviously we were meant to be together, right? I was caught up *again* and somehow, I forgot the past pains and conflicts.

After a pleasant season of reconnecting, our interactions changed and we eventually began to touch. I reasoned we sincerely cared for one another; in fact, we had real love that could not be forgotten or diluted with absence and distance. This other relationship of his was also changing so, I rationalized my position. In my heart we were betrothed to one another. Therefore our touching was ok. Marriage would just be a formality of what already existed. Hello… what fairy land did I move to? Our previous relationship had to mean something to him right? Initially I did not ask many questions because I told myself it would not even be happening if I had not ended our relationship. I was giving him space to do what he needed to do, right? Soon after we became intimate partners again, this other woman in his life became jealous and possessive and wanted to solidify her position in his life. She became so suspicious she would accuse him of wanting every woman who passed by, even if it was a woman they passed on the street. If an attractive woman passed their way, he would have to hear about it for the rest of the night. It was wearing on him. Well, guess what? I learned of these ongoing situations during our pillow talk. Imagine that. I am sure he told himself he was being honest and upfront, right? Remember he did tell me he had met someone but it was not serious, right? I wonder what he told her about me. Laugh out loud and roll over!

Near the end of this thing, in one of our conversations I asked him what he was doing and if this other relationship was growing, why did he continue to be involved with me. I heard the proverbial response phrased in a question, "What if I like yours better?" I asked who she was to him and if he referred to her as his girlfriend. He laughed as if joking and responded that she was. I felt really stupid and could not find the humor. I then asked, "Well who am I?" He gave me this huge grin and said "You are my girlfriend too." Was this supposed to be a joke? I beg your pardon. What...? Ring the alarm! Why didn't I call him ugly names and hit him as many of my sister friends would have? I referred to her as the other woman when in actuality; I had become the other woman. I was caught up and did not know how I would stop.

After this dialogue I knew it had to end... again. I felt so embarrassed. It felt shameful. That is just what I felt, dirty, used, and shameful. I felt ashamed because I allowed this to happen to me again. I know I allowed him back into my life. I was open and wanted things to be different; I wanted it to work out between us. What had changed with him other than the fact we had broken up and were apart for a few years? How had he grown? Yes, I let him back in; yet, I still acknowledged his contribution to what I was feeling. I did it to myself but he definitely played a role in the pain.

In the following week, he informs me she has moved in with him. When I heard those words, I felt like I had been stabbed in the back multiple times with an ice pick and then thrown onto the tracks of an approaching train. I realized they were building a relationship and I was just a play-mate. My pain and anger were indescribable. Again I had taken him for his word and also decided to ignore the information about the significance of the presence of the other woman in his life, even if it was "not serious." I did not ask the questions because I wanted to believe our love was powerful and he would do the right thing and choose me. My wise friend Rowena told me she will never compete for affection. I was not consciously aware I was in a competition but I was and I was also in denial. Rowena says. "Once you are in a competition for a man's affection or attention, you have already lost. You will never be able to leave that position until you leave the relationship."[6] I knew I had to leave the relationship again. Was this his pay-back because I previously ended the relationship and hurt him? I felt used and so incredibly stupid. In essence, I had to come to terms with the fact I did this to myself. He could not do anything to me or with me without my consent.

A greater part of me thanks God for Grayson because of our delirious experience. Because of our relationship and the hopelessness I felt when it was truly over, I had no place to turn but to him, Abba Father. As strange as it may sound, this event was one of the best things to ever happen to me. This was the darkest season of my life and I made it through. Even though I had rededicated my life back to God, I did not know him in the ways I experienced him through this brokenness. I never thought of taking my life; but there were many times I thought, if I did not have to inhale after my last exhalation it would be ok. I wanted the pain to go away. Looking back now, I can see

I had been visited by the spirit of depression, which crept in through the open door heartbreak left behind. I made it through with cycles of intense prayer, unrestrained crying, feasting on T D Jakes Ministries, and Bible study with a new purpose. I began to learn about and experience the Word of God in my life in new amazing ways. Listen, Observe, Ask, & Verify: *LOAV.* If you LOAV someone it will determine your capacity to LOVE them. LOAV them first.

Toby

Let me tell you about Mr. Toby, another unavailable man. I met Toby during what I would call a quiet time in my life. I had settled the fact that my last relationship was completely over without any hope of any part of it being salvaged. My ex and I had finally settled somewhere in the friends category as we both managed to move on. This was not like friends with benefits. As a matter of fact I was in the third year of an intentionally chosen season of abstinence, when I met Toby. I refocused my sexual energy into projects, worship, work, my family and working out at the gym. The real victory[7] was not by my efforts but by Grace, I was able to contain and discipline myself because of His love for me.

My girlfriends did not know how I did it, because they could not imagine being sexually inactive for that long. Anyway, right in the middle of this span of time, when I felt balanced, in waltzed Mr. Toby. Toby stands about 6' 3" and 220 pounds: tall, dark, and handsome, with great teeth, clean fingernails, and good shoes. I know it sounds strange but these are the things I was taught to look for. My brief encounter with Toby caused an intense emotional response that felt surreal almost as if something had overtaken me.

Meeting Toby

I was a Recruiter for a local marketing firm and our first conversation occurred in December of that year, before the holiday rush. He was an Account Manager for a regional advertising company and my firm was launching a new line of products and services. Toby was interested in creating a partnership that would allow his company to become the primary vendor for temporary and contractual marketing and graphic design staff. This would be a great contract for him. We spoke by phone and agreed to meet in the New Year when work flow for most people was more stable and new projects deadlines had been disclosed. I asked him to give me a call back in a few months when I would have more details and scope of the upcoming projects. He was diligent and called to set up a meeting after the hustle and bustle of the holiday season calmed.

Immediately, I found him attractive but was not sure if I was actually attracted to him. The ladies in the office teased about the tall, dark, and handsome visitor. The meeting went well and I considered using his services. Within the week, he scheduled another meeting to introduce me to the Customer Service Manager who would be my main point of contact. Valerie would be my direct point of contact and off-site manager of the temporary staff who would be reporting for work.

He seemed to be friendlier in this second meeting than when he came alone. It became obvious he was attracted to me. After consulting with my manager to negotiate the details and getting the approval to proceed, we signed agreements to seal the deal. To celebrate this new order of business, he invited me to lunch. Lunch with a business partner was not out of the ordinary; but I felt a strange little something in the pit of my belly. We went to an upscale Chinese restaurant for our first lunch meeting. Lunch was nice and open as we became more acquainted with each other and our perspective companies.

On the way back to the office, the energy in the car began to feel a little spicy. The way he looked at me when I got out of the car made me a little confused, uncomfortable, and excited. He was clearly wearing a wedding band, in plain sight. But there was something extra in the way he shook my hand when we parted. I had not been on a date for some time and he became more interesting by the minute. His personality complimented mine in so many ways. He was a talker and communicator; he was outgoing, and smart. He likes to read and travel. Like me, he enjoyed connecting with people and he seemed to really care about people.

The next week he called and asked me on another lunch "appointment." I started to get a little suspicious about his motives but it was fun, he was fun and I told myself it was not hurting anyone or anything so why not. It was business right? The next lunch meeting was at a small Italian restaurant. A few years back, I completed a course and became a Certified Reflexologist. I was thrilled about this form of art that actually helps people heal from many ailments. Anyway, providing a sample of Reflexology would also give me a little more insight into his physical and energetic condition. As we were waiting for our meal, I reached over and took his hand into my hands. He quickly pulled his hand back and asked what I just did to him. I had not done anything to him. He did give his hand back and I proceeded to explain the philosophy of Reflexology and how it works. I gave him a sample of Hand Reflexology. There was definitely a spark and connection from this point in our communicating. After this meeting, I knew I would like to see him again, even though I knew danger signs were approaching. I felt a tug from the spirit realm that was hypnotic and subtly erotic; and, I knew it was not safe. So I called my aunt, my confidant. She is a loving partner available to walk with me through difficult times, events, and decisions in my life.

I explained all that happened. We talked and I prayed and she prayed too. At that time I gave God permission to help me. I gave him permission to intervene, to interfere, to control my life because I felt those old familiar sensations and thoughts and I knew I was headed toward trouble I did not want to turn away from.

In the meetings and conversations to come, I learned of Toby's supposed challenges at home. I am certain he cared for his wife and family. From his statements, he felt more of an obligation to her family than a love and passion for her (So he said). Her family had been there for him when his own family was not available.

According to him, his wife's personality was very opposite of his and mine. He lead me to believe he was not intellectually, emotionally, or physically satisfied. He perceived I was a person who could meet those needs. He acknowledged his own internal battle with our connection. Now we were not talking about sex yet but let me tell you it was definitely in our thoughts. I made sure I capitalized on every meeting by being as attractive as I could be. As a professional, I always dressed professionally. I did not show any skin and I did not wear anything too tight; but, I managed to pick my sexiest professional attire when I knew I would be seeing him. Sexy is not about how much skin you show or what you reveal. I wanted to give him something to think about (Terrible!). Our next meeting took place after hours at a cozier establishment. On this particular occasion the young lady who waited on us, thought we were a couple. In our meetings we were getting to know each other. I heard about his sisters, their families and struggles. Toby shared his fears and childhood pains. I learned about his sons who are his motivation and driving force to be successful in life. I learned his wife was special to him in an enduring kind of way and not a passionate way (Really?). I was asking questions, just not the right ones.

The next week, I requested a meeting. I needed to have some questions answered. We did not talk about personal things during business hours and I did not contact him during the evening hours. It is crazy how we just fall into place and do what we are not supposed to do, so well. I felt a turn in my heart. I began to believe I really cared for this person and I needed to know if I was alone. I wanted to know what he was feeling and thinking about me. Excuse my language, #!@! but what was I thinking? What happened to me, what did I eat or do to allow myself to be approaching this place again? I mean look at my history. I should have known better! I could not rationalize this. What about my strong relationship with the Father? Ahh, the human condition is quite complicated.

We met for lunch. Keep in mind, throughout this time I felt divided but I was still headed down this path toward this man who was not available. I told myself some unspoken lie and accepted it. When you keep heading in a direction that you know is wrong you have given yourself permission to proceed or you would stop the progression. However, even though I was headed in the wrong direction, I never stopped sending up petitions to the Father to help me. I was being distracted. I wanted to do the right thing but I was also very hungry if you know what I mean. It was in my head and I wanted it; I wanted him.

We met during lunch at a coffee shop. He confirmed and confessed he was thinking and feeling all of the things I was thinking and feeling. He wanted to spend some special private time with me as well. He did say he had never done this before. He claimed no one had caused him to feel like this before. The conversation was not explicit: yet, after this conversation I began to feel as if our desires had been consummated as if we had done the deed, even though we had only touched hands. We had an exchange of energy as we sat sipping our coffee and green tea. Energy is powerful thing!

We never shared a kiss or even an inappropriate hug because we always met in public places. This was an unconscious form of protection. We had not made actual plans to get together, just plans to make plans. But, this Friday's meeting was different. I was strangely satisfied as if this meeting completed something. Knowing the end of the road had arrived and danger and doom were eminent. There was nothing else to talk about; it was time to set a date to do the deed.

That night, I went to the Father one more time and pleaded with him to help me. I did not feel in control of my thoughts or actions. Like Hezekiah on his death bed[8] I put God in remembrance of me. I reminded Him I had given him full permission with me, to help me. I also reminded Him of the good things I had done following his lead. I knew I belonged to Him but my operating system was having technical difficulty. I sincerely wanted to do the right thing. As you are reading this, I know you are thinking about the last poor decisions I made in the prior relationships I shared. Toby and I had no history for me to rationalize. Was I really going to do this thing that would be the most mindless thing I had ever done? It was clear right up front, he was not available. I should not have even entertained the idea. How did it get into my head anyway? Was my guard down? My mental software had been compromised with some type of Trojan virus and I needed professional help! Friday night, I sent up one more S.O.S for help and went to bed.

The next morning I woke with complete clarity. AMEN! I was delivered from this desire **completely**, overnight. His name or thoughts of him did not stir me in any way. It was amazing and beautiful! I felt saved, rescued, freed; and I know who had done it for me. I knew I was free from this obsession and meditation which had now gone on for about eight weeks. My petition for help was granted. We did not meet for lunch or anything else again. Our business conversations were friendly but focused. He never asked me what changed or why I changed my mind. How could he? He was in no position to be concerned about me and my affairs. After all, he was not even a real friend. A few years passed and I had accepted another job opportunity. I called him to get current information on his company. He answered because he did not recognize the number. Interestingly enough, he responded he was out having drinks with a friend. Imagine that.

With Parker I was unsuspecting and very naive. With Grayson I was hopeful and filled with such memories and emotions of an intense love that over powered my better judgment. With Toby, it was a surprise but I was no longer naive and we did not have any history which often complicates emotions and decisions, as with Grayson. I was wrong. I knew better; but my heart and my body wanted something different. I did not know Parker was lying. Somewhere inside of me I knew Grayson loved me even though we had to end. The difference is I wanted to believe Toby because it felt good. I wanted the attention. I wanted to be touched. I wanted to be wanted and the chemistry was strong. I believe Toby was referred to me by a Mr. Lou Cipher. You see, Lou knew all the things I just mentioned I wanted when I did not consciously know I was missing those things, until Toby walked in.

I was delivered form this awaiting train wreck by Grace, alone. My heart was truly willing to do the right thing so Grace could come in. If you find yourself in this situation, no matter how bad you feel about what you should not be feeling or should not be doing, do not ever stop talking to God. He is there as an ever present help in your time of need[9] or trouble no matter what type of trouble it could be. He is waiting for you to call on Him.[10] Today, I heard part of a sermon by Bishop Jakes that spoke directly to my victory. It was part of a series called Save the Scraps. Relaying what our Water Walking Jesus was trying to tell us, Bishop said, "If you don't invite me into your situation, you will never see me snatch you out of a situation you enjoyed being in."[11] We need to be in constant remembrance of past success and miracles to know the very proof of a past miracle holds the probability and proof of current and future miracles and deliverance. It is through asking[12] and inviting God into our situations that enables him to snatch or rescue us from the messes we have intentionally or unintentionally created. I was headed into the wrong direction into a situation I fantasized and began to meditate on, but I never stopped inviting my God into my situation. And He saved me! He saved me from Me! I escaped this near tragedy.

I cannot with a good conscious attempt to apply LOAV to this affair with Toby; and, that is exactly what it was. We never did the wild monkey dance. We only touched hands how innocent is that?

It was not innocent at all. You see, you do not have to have sex to have an affair or cheat on your partner. He cheated on his wife with me and I sadly confess I was a participant. He gave me energy, thoughts, information, and emotional interaction which should have been reserved for his wife. Cheating does not begin with sex; it begins in the mind with thoughts and words which generate the initial emotional infidelity that often leads to sex. This is another reason it is so important to learn to manage our thoughts and emotions and not allow them to rule or mange us.

I was so fortunate and blessed to have this situation end before any sexual contact. Emotional infidelity is definitely magnified when sex becomes a part of the dynamics. These types of situations usually never end without causing significant injury to definitely one if not both participants. We are worth so much more than what these situations offer. Do not deceive yourself. You can be in control of you, with the right guidance and help.

I had given Parker and Grayson access to my heart, my mind, my time, and eventually my body. No, it was not against my will; but it was against sound knowledge and understanding exactly what I was surrendering or what I would gain by the surrender. It does not happen all at one time but it can happen quickly. I did not know them well enough to invest and share my commodities the ways I did. Toby never gained access to my body but he definitely did spend a lot of time in my head.

My Advice

If you find yourself tiptoeing around a scenario like any of these you have just read, stop in your tracks!

- Check your thoughts and emotions.
- Tell yourself the Truth about your situation.
- Tell yourself the Truth about what you are considering.
- Share it with a real friend who sincerely cares for you.
- Pray, lace up your sneakers and prepare to run, pray again, and run like the wind.

The truth about any kind of scenario with a married man regardless of what you have justified is there are not any conditional exclusions, which would ever make it acceptable or appropriate at any time. If you decide to take a taste or even a single sip of this type of indulgence it will dissolve your ability to make the right choice. The best way to avoid these dreadful circumstances is to plan ahead. You cannot wait until you get into a situation to determine what you will do or how you will behave; real life does not work that way. You have to plan a defense strategy and a route of escape beforehand.

Think about it, every commonly known safety measure requires some form of drill or practice to be effective. Our schools and businesses across the country conduct a variety of drills including fire, hurricane, and earthquake drills, bomb threat evacuations, high school safety lockdowns, and terrorist safety drills. All of these practices designate certain signs to look for to determine the specifics of the danger or threat. After the danger has been identified, there are steps which must be taken in an immediate and orderly fashion. These steps lead to forms of escape and survival requiring people to ask for help and work together through the crisis. Plans also include the process of regrouping, reconnecting, and accounting for all individuals involved. In real world, best case scenarios allow you to go home and hug and kiss your families. In the worst cases there may be loss and fatalities. You may have to learn you have to accept a new reality and begin a new life without people you cherish. The only way to get through these types of life storms is to have a plan.

Likewise, you need a predetermined plan as to how you will handle potential and existing relationships. You need a detailed blueprint of what you require for survival and what you can live without. Predetermine what you will and will not accept, as it pertains to your most valuable possession, you. Resolve and record your beliefs and standards and review them on a regular basis. It would not be a bad idea to share them with a few esteemed friends. This will prepare you to take action to protect and maintain your beliefs and standards. Sharing also adds accountability supports; if you should slip and fall, a friend would help you get up and stay with you until you are stabilized.

You cannot create an effective strategy for defense and preservation in the middle of any storm or crisis. Establish your resources, strength, and methodologies before an emergency or crisis happens. You may never have to execute a real life performance, however you will be prepared if you are called to action. For example, if you are trained in CPR, how many times have you had to use it? Good to know, right?

US Militaries would be completely ineffective if they did not practice what they are expected to perform. The same goes for all recreational and professional athletes, artists, performers, and academics. Everything in our lives requires planning and practice. Why would we think our stuff and our relationships should be excluded? If you want something to work out for you, you better plan and practice for it. It is all about training. Devise a plan and think of it as your Relationship and Risk Management Strategy (RRMS). Part of my personal relationship risk management process requires me to stay on guard whenever I am in the presence of unavailable men. I become very aware of my presence, my feeling, the conversations, my body language, and my intentions. After having a few victories and feeling safe and comfortable, in walked a Mr. Toby. I have resolved this will not happen to me again.

Stop - Look - & Listen
Stop in your tracks!
Stop all movement and be still.
Look into your heart, your mind, and your emotions.
Look into the truth about what you are considering and the ramifications.
Look into the pain and fears which might have brought you to this place.
Listen to good counsel.
Listen to the small still quite voice within you and receive your victory.

What I Discovered
I like to position myself to learn from all of my experiences. As a result of this desire I am continually engaging in introspective thoughts and activities. Looking back over my history of relationships, I began to uncover some clearly defined and not so pretty habits and tendencies. I needed to understand why I repeatedly found myself being involved with or entertaining thoughts of being with an unavailable man. My self-confidence has always been high. I don't ever remember a time when I did not like myself or a time of feeling unattractive. When I walk into a room, I expect to be noticed and acknowledged not for physical attributes but because of who I am. Of course during different seasons of my life I wished parts of me were clearer, larger or smaller; but I always liked me. I was athletic, funny, and smart; smart enough anyway. I didn't take myself too seriously and was always accused of wearing rosy colored glasses and smiling too much.

I wanted some answers to why my relationships were not as successful as they could be. I began to examine all of my past relationships as far back as I could remember. There was a time in my younger years when I was a no-nonsense kind of girl who had zero tolerance for any form or suspicion of infidelity. In my first year of high school, my boyfriend went to a football game I wasn't able to make. The news got back to me, he was extremely flirtatious and fooling around with some girl at the game. I called his house before he got home and spoke with his sister. I told her to tell him I heard about what he was up to and he never needed to call me again. I never gave him a chance to tell me what happened and this was the end of our relationship. Prior to this time, I was the designated protector of my younger sisters. I would beat-up anyone who bothered them and I was the bully of bullies. I could never idly stand by while someone was being bullied and hurt without cause. It did not matter to me; I would fight a boy or a girl on the spot.

Please know as I continue, I am not trying to put my family's secrets on blast, but if my truth can help you, you can have it. My father was shipped off to the Vietnam War when I was a baby. As you know war had traumatizing effects on all soldiers. When he returned, previous marital conflicts were compounded by the new issues created by the war. It wasn't long before his relationship with my mother crumbled. This relationship ended in divorce. When I became a young lady, my mother told me about my father's extramarital activities; infidelity was the ultimate reason the marriage ended. Take note, my father's parents were divorced during a time when divorce was not so popular. Did I have missing daddy issues? Maybe, but I don't believe I wasn't looking for my father in relationships; because, I had many positive male models in my life. A few years after my parents divorced my mother remarried. I grew up in a stable two parent household. My step-father adopted me to make our family complete and official. My mother was an Educator and my father an Attorney. I have great family and childhood memories; however, at some point infidelity came to visit us again. Unfortunately, as a teenager, I learned about affairs both of my parents were involved in. Yes this marriage also ended in divorce.

My step-father's parents were divorced and his father later married the woman who came between him and his wife. There were stories about my grandfather, my mother's father, and the possibility of him having "outside children." By this time, I also heard about my great grandfather who's nick name was Red Fox. Red Fox was married to my great grandmother and was caught running for safety without his pants, when his woman's husband chased him with a shot gun. When we first hear and picture these types of stories most of us laugh. It sounds funny on a superficial level. Actually these sad stories cause great pain and chaos within families. It might be funny in the movies, but it is not so funny in real life. What my parents went through was painful for all of us. In one way or another, my siblings and I are still dealing with the repercussions today. With infidelity and divorce, no one wins, everyone loses.

I too had a few issues. I was not a saint. In one relationship, I became unfaithful after being wounded by an unfaithful partner. Somehow my indiscretion did not fix our problem or make me feel any better about anything.

As I dug deeper, I concluded I behaved the way I did due to what my parents and family modeled for me. **Modeling is irresistibly powerful.** Modeling produces results based on the content of what is being modeled. Even if you consciously do not agree with what's being done, the seed has been planted. If it happens repeatedly over time, you have a lot of seeds and one day one of those seeds is likely to come up. Unhealthy relationships were modeled for me from a young age. I was unaware of the affect other family relationships were having on me and my future relationship choices. I was unaware of what the real choices were. Our children are more attuned to what we do rather than what we say. We hear it all the time, "actions speak louder than words."

Modeling is one of the loudest and most effective forms of teaching and communicating.

If you are a parent, what are you saying to your children with you actions, inactions, and compromises? In my family the acceptance and participation in unfaithful activities is an example of an unattractive hand-me down, passed from generation to generation.

I grew excited by this revelation; I had some answers but I was not completely satisfied with the Modeling Theory alone. I could not stop my research with just accepting the concept of modeling, because I felt there had to be more. I did not throw out the modeling theory but I did add to it. The overarching issue I and my family had, and I am saying had because I don't have it any more, is iniquity by way of infidelity and divorce. As I just described the damaging operations of my own family tree, infidelity was the big elephant in our homes, no one truly talked about. People told stories about others family members but not about themselves and their own struggles. You cannot fix what's broken or not working properly if you don't talk about it. Iniquity does not discriminate; it is an equal opportunity business entity. My mother has married a few times and my white daddies and black daddies had this problem. This same iniquity was in their family trees as well. Birds of a feather do flock together. There is an increased likelihood you draw or will be attracted to people who share you challenges good and bad. My mother was attracted and drawn to men who also had a similar "infidelity-divorce iniquity gene." To solve, cure, or end this type of issue you must pursue spiritual guidance. Traditional helpers and counselors can design great treatment plans to help you heal and repair the damage infidelity causes; however, you need spiritual resources to address iniquity. You must invite Jesus into your counseling sessions if you sincerely want true deliverance. Infidelity iniquity is a generational spiritual problem and it is the root cause of relationship dysfunction regardless of the expression. Other expressions include emotional and physical abuse, molestation, mean spiritedness, oppression, and a variety of addictions.

I had the personality traits and the confidence to refuse to accept these types of relationships but it seemed I was unable to avoid them. On some level I accepted infidelity was just something people did. If you love someone you don't just leave them because they make a mistake right? It is not a simple mistake and it is a big deal. The sacredness of marriage and sex makes it a huge deal. Married military officials and celebrities are ridiculed and demoted when caught in compromised sexual situations with single and married partners who are not their spouses. The military severely punishes individuals caught being unfaithful to their spouses and if proven guilty he or she could even spend time in jail. Infidelity is also the only reason Jesus allows for divorce. It is a serious offense with the state and the church. Shouldn't we take a closer look at why it is so serious? What does this offense do to our families, relationships and how we see ourselves? **I am not** advocating that women who are married and have built families should call it quits for their husband's mistakes and judgment failures. I repeat life is complicated and your choices are between you and God. Do not go and tell anyone Princess told you to do anything! What I am advocating for is, as women we must get to know our men, their habits, personality traits, and family histories before we start sharing our hearts, mind, body, and time with them. We must get to know our men before we become their lovers and definitely before becoming their wives. Let us not make a mockery of the divine and immensely sacred institution of marriage. For me, freedom was in the middle of finding these answers to my relationship challenges. I am free to choose and free to be cherished. I will share more about the cherished part later, in chapter 13. By the way, my mother has also learned the power of choice and her life is also better. What information do you need to uncover and explore your family tree to find your freedom?

REFLECTIONS

Take a few moments and think about your past relationships. Do you have a Parker, Grayson, or Toby in your past? Consider what you will need to in order to avoid potential or future unavailable men. Take out your journal and answer some important questions about your relationships. Start with self-analysis and apply the LOAV Method and consider your RRMS.

Start with answering these questions:

What excess baggage do you need to clear up in your life?
What are three rules you need to make about your stuff today?
What can you live with and what can you not live without?
What patterns do you see in your relationship history?
How does unfaithfulness affect our families, relationships and how we see ourselves?
What is the major problem you and your family face in relationships?

Apply the LOAV Method to your present or previous relationships.

RRMS. Consider measures you need to have in place to avoid unavailable men. Record at least 3 measures or steps for your personal Relationship Risk Management Strategy (RRMS) regarding unavailable men.

4

Non-Family Men

Most women want children and families because we were created and wired with this desire[1]. If you have taken the time to pursue a career, you have probably heard the mention of a clock and racing against time. Some of us already have children and families and are looking to create successful blended families.

What would we do without our family supports? We would not have joy in our lives if we are constantly warring with the most important people to us, our families. If a gentleman has a poor relationship with his mother, there is an increased likelihood he has poor relationships with all women in his life. The mother-child relationship is one of the most powerful connections we will experience in life. Mothers are the initial primary teachers and conveyers of communication, survival, and learning skills. If he resents his mother or was abused by her in anyway, he may eventually resent you. You will be the person to pay for his abuse and pain if he does not find healing and deliverance.

If he doesn't like children or want children, chances are, he was raised in an environment that did not value him or provide his basic needs. You cannot give or provide what you have never received. If he was not loved and cared for, he will be unable to truly love and care for others. If he feels he was cheated in his youth, he might think someone owes him, and may be consciously or unconsciously out to get even or get back at you, his new target. If he believes abortion is a birth control option, he might influence you to eliminate one of our future leaders, scientists, doctors, teachers, or mothers. Just think we would still be waiting to see the miracle of the election of President Obama if his mother had been influenced to have an abortion.

If he is continually at odds with his family and speaks negatively of them, where is his loyalty? Would you expect him to be loyal to you? How could he be? Maybe he doesn't want the responsibility because of insufficiency in his own experience. Maybe he was abused and fears he has potential to become the abuser. Where does he spend the holidays and with whom? Holidays can present very challenging family moments and some of the best memories of our lives. You need to know all these things before you start sharing your stuff with him.

Would you intentionally and knowingly start a relationship you know does not have a chance to succeed? If we are here for relationships, family relationships must be supported. If a man really cares about you, at some point he will be willing to introduce you to his friends and family. If not something is wrong with him or something is wrong with them. A selfish man is not typically interested in family operations either. He will probably not designate adequate quality time for you or your children because he is too self-absorbed. Do not automatically assume because a man has children, he's a family man. He could have children all around the city and not be a man to any of the women he was with or a father to any of the children he helped create. I know you have heard the song *Papa was a Rollin' Stone*[2]. We know he could not have been a very good Papa.

Be careful of a man who shows an excessive affinity for your family too soon. One man in my life took a liking to one of my sisters. This affinity was not obvious at first. One night after I had gone to bed, I noticed he was still up. When I went down stairs I saw he was still up and working on a writing project. As I approached he crumbled the last page and tossed it toward the trash can. After realizing how late it was he came up to bed. While cleaning up the next morning, I noticed a few crumpled papers. Right before tossing one of them into the trash, for some reason I decided to un-crumple one and read it.

My heart skipped a beat as I began to read a beautiful and sensual poem about my sister. I was never angry with my sister because she had absolutely nothing do with this situation and his issues. She was currently in a relationship with a man who seemed to make her happy. I confronted him with the poem; he pleaded for forgiveness. This kind of issue has the ability to destroy family relationships. I never shared this with my sister and needless to say, the relationship eventually ended.

On a different note, if a man is married to his job, wants to spend more time with his buddies than with you, never has time for family gatherings, or anything fun, chances are he is a Non-Family man. Leave him be. You will not be able to change him. The change might come later but it must be generated from within him.

Preston

Preston was a good guy. He is refined. He loves to travel and has a great appreciation for diverse cultural expressions. His challenge is with family. Preston struggled with friendships of all forms because of the negative experiences with his family. He did not have solid friendships with other guys or even stable platonic friendships with women. No, he is not gay. When his new girlfriend Kendall, asked about meeting his friends, he really did not have any. He had one long distance friend he spoke with on occasion; but he did not have any local friends to share the things guys share. Ladies, don't let guys fool you. They do talk to each other and of course some talk more than others, guys do kiss and tell. After being on his current job for over a decade, he still did not have any regular or meaningful connections with his co-workers.

Kendall thought meeting his friends would provide a greater insight of the real Preston. Preston's other issue was his lack of family connection. He would often speak of how manipulative his mother was and there were times when she would stop speaking to him. She had a tumultuous past and even suffered from mental health issues and had a diagnosis of clinical depression.

Preston's father was often harsh with him and caused him to become preoccupied with the fears of failure and letting him down, and the constant struggle to please him. These pressures to perform lead to immobilizing feelings of inadequacy. Being referred to as the "asshole," by his father did not help. Standards set by his parents would cause him to attempt to perform their wishes or go into hiding. And this became his pattern and it spilled over into all of his relationships.

Additional family confusion was revealed when Kendall realized Preston's ex-wife was closer to his parents than he was. In a way she was a like a spy for them. She kept them abreast of everything he did or did not do. His mother even went behind his back and returned the wedding rings to his ex-wife after the divorce. His ex-wife previously tried to pawn them; but since the diamond was registered she was unable to do so. He was forced to buy them back from her along with many other personal items she confiscated. Because he continued to delay introducing Kendall to his parents she never had a formal introduction even after dating him for a year.

Kendall's man was a Non-Family man. Family was not good to him and he had not learned how to create new family and have real connections and relationships. There are a lot of questions he needs to ask and have answered. He is a great person to know, he was good to her and handy around the house. He even repaired many things in her home. He would even spend time with her son, by taking him to concerts, sporting events, and talking to him about man stuff.

As good as he is, he is not ready for a real relationship and surely needs to get some counseling. He has family issues which need to be resolved before he could be an important equation in a healthy relationship.

Take a closer look at this list.

THE NON-FAMILY MEN LIST

Do NOT give YOUR STUFF to a man who does not like his mother.
Do NOT give YOUR STUFF to a man who does not like children.
Do NOT give YOUR STUFF to a man who supports abortion as a birth control option.
Do NOT give YOUR STUFF to a man who speaks negatively of his sisters.
Do NOT give YOUR STUFF to a man who does not love his family.

Do NOT give YOUR STUFF to a man who will not introduce his family.

Do NOT give YOUR STUFF to a man who does not have any friends.

Do NOT give YOUR STUFF to a man who will not discipline his children.

Do NOT give YOUR STUFF to a man who is not willing to spend quality time with his children.

Do NOT give YOUR STUFF to a man who does not fulfill his child support obligations.

Do NOT give YOUR STUFF to a man who is not compassionate.

Do NOT give YOUR STUFF to a man who is not serving the God you serve.

Do NOT give YOUR STUFF to a man who has no religion.

Do NOT give YOUR STUFF to a selfish man.

REFLECTIONS

Take a few moments and think about your past relationships. Do you have a Preston in your past? Consider what you will need to avoid potential non-family men. Take your journal and answer some important questions about your relationships

Questions

What complications did or would a non-family man bring into your life?

What are three rules you need to protect you from this type of relationship?

What are the issues of this kind of relationship you could live without?

Apply the LOAV Method to your non-family man if applicable.

RRMS. Consider measures you need to have in place to avoid non-family men Record at least 3 measures or steps for your personal Relationship Risk Management Strategy (RRMS) regarding non-family men.

5

Man-Child Men

Another name for a Man-Child is a Boy. I am not intending to be derogatory in any way. One type of a Man-Child is a male who is actually young in age and inexperienced in life. As a young man, he may have great potential; however, he still lives at home with his mother or parents, is not gainfully employed, depends on his family's financial support, and does not have a plan for his future. He may be charismatic and have an awesome personality. He may talk a good game and be quite the intellectual, however, the last time I checked these qualities do not pay the bills.

Do not rule him out or give up on him, he still has time to get it together. Just don't give him your stuff until he does or you will be the one to pay for his mistakes or short comings. Another type of Man-Child is actually the older version of the young one who never figured things out. More than likely, he has had a few hurtful experiences which have trapped him in time and development. He will not be able to grow or evolve just because you decide to give him your good stuff. He actually needs some professional, spiritual, and vocational assistance. Stay away until you know for sure he has been delivered. Don't let him talk you out of your stuff. He cannot and will not be able to provide what you need for a rewarding and healthy relationship.

Sebastian

Let us do a little back-tracking now as I introduce you to Sebastian. Now unlike the Man-Child described above, Sebastian was not a dead beat and he did have a plan for his future; we were just too young to handle these types of adult issues. When I went off to college, I experienced what I would consider my first real "adult-acting" relationship. I felt more grown up and in control of my life. Sebastian and I could spend time together without considering the opinions of our parents.

My parents were hundreds of miles away and his parents were two states away. Although we did not live together, I did have my own apartment. Translation: we were able to play like grown-ups. This new life was beautiful and the introduction of this thing called sex was absolutely amazing. I could not get enough of it. Since I was all grown up I decided I was ready to become sexually active and Sebastian was my man. Being as smart as I thought I was, I knew I would have to get some form of contraceptive or birth control. Initially, I tried the pill; however, I did not like the bloated feeling or the weight gain symptoms it created for me. Next, I tried the diaphragm. It was a little messy but I thought it worked until the day my monthly cycle (Judy) failed to show up. At first I was not alarmed. I thought the stress of life and busyness delayed it. It became apparent, Judy had stopped visiting me and was not going to return any time soon. I was pregnant.

After receiving positive test results, I called Sebastian and give him the news. He did not have a great response in either direction. What's a young girl to do when this happens? This is a conversation I should have initiated in person and not on the phone, a regular phone. We did not own cell phones back then. It should not be communicated by texting, or any other form of social media.

I eventually talked to my mother and she assured me she loved me and she would support whatever decision I made. I also talked to Sebastian's mother. I can remember the conversation so clearly; she approved of me and loved me. Barbara told me I had to make the most selfish decision of my life. She told me, she and Sebastian Sr. would love to be grandparents; but she could not make the decision for me. She went on to explain, ultimately the pregnancy to term and the responsibility of caring for a new person would be on me as the new mother, regardless of how much others would say they would help.

I spoke to another woman, Towanda, who told me the quickening does not happen until the end of the first trimester. She was in essence telling me, I was carrying a fetus that did not have a soul yet. She believed the soul would enter the fetus, at the end of the third month. Today, I know this is not true, I was misinformed. A few weeks passed since we initially received the news. I remember talking with Sebastian about our options; but, he never spoke of what he would like to have happen. He was always silent whenever the topic came up. Eventually I had to make a decision. With all the information I had received and no input from him, I decided to terminate the pregnancy. I really did not want to do it alone. I did not want to become a single parent at 20. I always wanted to have children but not like that. We were so young and still in college. We were still dependents needing our parents to take care of us. Marriage was something for our future and not something we were interested in at the time. He had not asked me to marry him. He did not relay any ideas suggesting he would be supportive or involved if I gave birth to our child.

I heard about a few classmates who had this procedure and went right back to school. It's my body and I have the right to do what I want to with it right? It is my right isn't it? Did I really believe this? As the story goes, I followed through with the procedure and had an abortion. I talked with a counselor, watched a short video, and signed some papers. I was so afraid and wanted to change my mind; but,

I was caught up in the decision and process and did not know how to stop it. When the procedure was over, I remember looking around the room for some form of evidence of what just happened or some proof of my pregnancy. They were very careful to not allow me to see anything. I received a valium in recuperation. It was done.

Later that evening, Sebastian came to visit me at my aunt's house. My family left us alone so we could have some privacy and time to talk. I told him what I went through and all that had happened. He asked if I was ok. He then said something that blew my mind. He said he was hoping I would have told him, I did not go through with it. Inside my head, I began to scream, shout, and convulse, while my face reflected calmness and composure. I had nothing to say to his comment. He had nothing to share throughout this process and now he says something like that. I never knew he cared. Maybe he thought he did not or should not have a say in what I should or should not do. Had I known he cared, I believe my choice would have been different; I loved him. Even if we came to the same decision, I would not have felt so alone in the process. Now, I am not blaming him for my decision. I made the decision but I made a decision with insufficient information or input for him. We were children, he was a child. He was not a man.

He was not in any position to provide for me and a baby. Could we have been more careful? Probably, but the truth is, pregnancy is always a possibility when you are sexually active with healthy and functional reproductive organs. Young or old, if you are in a non-married and non-committed relationship, you need to know if the man in your equation is willing and capable of providing for you and your possible children. If you become pregnant, is he prepared and willing to fill this role? You should not marry someone who cannot provide for you or your children.

Porsche's Story

Porsche is a beautiful creative and smart woman. Unfortunately she does not know it. At least she didn't when I met her. She is now learning the true value and who she is. She is working diligently on discovering and exploring her lovable, worthy, and authentic self. Curiously, Porsche sees herself as a "Daddy's girl." Most Daddies' girls receive an extra element of confidence or validation through the type of nurturing only a father can provide. She was the apple of his eye, yet the world has continually worked hard at destroying the beauty of her reflection through his eyes. She recounts numerous stories of being told she was not good enough, attractive enough or curvy enough. She was always too skinny or too light. Somewhere in the course of life, she began to believe these lies. The fact that she could be a runway super model doesn't matter. It does not matter that after puberty her body matured and blessed her with perfect measurements. The body she now has is what women are paying plastic surgeons to design.

Porsche experienced several failed relationships. One of the relationships actually led to a marriage that did not have a fighting chance, because of his and her soul wounds. As a result of this union, she had two children Samantha and Timothy. After defeating what would have been diagnosed as depression, she moved from Detroit to Phoenix hoping to move away from her pain and sadness and begin a fresh start in a new town with her children.

The new start was good. Struggling to establish her independence and self-sufficiency was not easy; however, she began to enjoy the feelings of accomplishment. She had a few good friends, attended social events and had landed a great job. Everything was looking up. Could it get any better? Samantha was a few years older than her brother and involved in many extra circular activities. It was now time for Timothy to have an opportunity to begin participating in sports to learn where his interests and talents might take him. She registered Tim for a youth recreational baseball team. He picked up the techniques of the game and quickly became one of the best players on the team. Simultaneously, the coach William began to express interest in getting to know Porsche on a more personal level.

William was also the owner of a small auto detailing business just outside of the city. He was doing quite well for himself. To attract her, he started with favors of providing transportation to and from practice for Timothy and spending extra time with him. He also began to detail her car, free of charge. When he started to ask her out, she could not imagine telling him she was not interested, after all he had done. According to her, he was not her type. Even so, Porsche started dating William. With his diligent pursuit, it did not take long before she began to develop deeper feeling for him.

Were they compatible? Did they have the same spiritual beliefs or views on disciplining children? How was he so successful and still available? Well, he was single though he had been married once before. There were no children from that union. He owned his home and was a pretty savvy business man. She did learn he had no interest in ever getting married. As he put it, he simply did not believe in marriage and would never get married again. Well what do you know? A few months later, she discovered she was pregnant again and moves in with him. This makes sense right? A part of her believed she could change him. She believed, because they created a family, he would change his views down the road. During the course of their relationship, she had two more children with him. One of her children was born a few months after the birth of another child, he had with another woman. Long story short, she discovered multiple affairs, more children, addiction to pornography, the use of prostitutes, abuse of alcohol, and gambling. These are the habits and addictions of an individual who does not have self-control, much like a child. He is a selfish man regardless of the root cause of his problems.

He moved her in and continued to have children with her and other women knowing he never wanted to get married. She was not his concern. He was only concerned with himself and his own needs. William looked like a man but he did not behave like one. He was ruled by senses and appetites and was not in pursuit of any spiritual elevation. Interestingly enough, his father was a Pastor. William needs to ask and answer many questions about his life's purpose. He was not the best choice for her especially with history of difficult relationships.

Porsche finally managed to muster up the strength to leave. Imagine the plunge of her current level of self-esteem, when she moved in with him. She had no idea who she decided to lay with. She deceived herself and was deceived by him. What could she have done differently or better? She wants to be truly loved and married someday. She cannot imagine another man would take her as his wife with five children. She is even more preoccupied with her appearance.

What happened here? She loved a man and gave away all of her stuff to a man who was not capable of loving her back. She gave away her time, her emotions, her body, her money and her love. She gave him all of her stuff. She began giving her stuff to him without taking the time to get to know who he was on the inside. Physical features, careers, and material possessions cannot compare in value to a man with integrity and honorable character.

When we are preparing to enter a partnership for business, or to purchase a home, or even to accept new employment, there are many forms and documents detailing pertinent information. The fine print details the restrictions and requirements for the partnership and the ensuring protocol designed for civil dissolution, in the event the partnership needs to end. Ladies, we need to create our own documents of restrictions and requirements for partnership and deny access to those who do not meet compliance. We need to know what we are getting involved in right up front, then we can make an educated decision and decide if we are in or out.

My aunt taught me the phrase of "Stop Loss." Stop going in the wrong direction and turn around. It is often much easier to bounce in the beginning. Early bouncing is a form of damage control. So what if you feel like you have made poor choices and wasted your time. If you learn from each experience, it is never a waste. If you chose to proceed without conducting your due diligence then you should prepare yourself for what will surely come. Go into perspective or potential relationships with your eyes wide open. Let me just say it is not all negative. You are looking for the good stuff too. Take steps to ensure your vision is balanced. Do not become so stuck and obsessed with negative traits and characteristics you never see the good ones.

Revisit the LOAV connection and apply it to her situation. Hurting and vulnerable people do not always make the best decisions.

What could or should she have done differently?

THE MAN-CHILD MEN LIST

Do NOT give YOUR STUFF to a man who is a boy.
Do NOT give YOUR STUFF to a man who cannot pay his own way.
Do NOT give YOUR STUFF to a man who does not want to work.
Do NOT give YOUR STUFF to a man who wants you to take care of him.
Do NOT give YOUR STUFF to a man whose mother takes care of him.
Do NOT give YOUR STUFF to a man who does not have any dreams or ambitions.
Do NOT give YOUR STUFF to a man who prefers spending time with his friends.
Do NOT give YOUR STUFF to a man who abuses his personal property.
Do NOT give YOUR STUFF to a man who does not fulfill his child support obligations.
Do NOT give YOUR STUFF to a man who cannot provide your needs.
Do NOT give YOUR STUFF to a man who does not have good hygiene.
Do NOT give YOUR STUFF to a man who is financially irresponsible.
Do NOT give YOUR STUFF to a man who chases get rich schemes.
Do NOT give YOUR STUFF to a selfish man.

REFLECTIONS

Take a few moments and think about your past relationships with a man-child. Do you have a Sebastian or a William in your history? Consider what you will need to avoid these and potential future man-child men. Take out your journal and answer some important questions about your relationships.

Questions

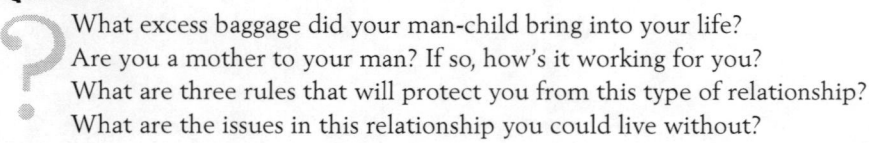

What excess baggage did your man-child bring into your life?
Are you a mother to your man? If so, how's it working for you?
What are three rules that will protect you from this type of relationship?
What are the issues in this relationship you could live without?

Apply the LOAV Method to your man-child relationships if applicable.

RRMS. Consider measures you need to have in place to avoid man-child men. Record at least 3 measures or steps for your personal Relationship Risk Management Strategy (RRMS) regarding man-child men.

6

Off Limits Men

If you want to avoid unnecessary complications in daily living, stay away from the Off Limits Man. The men on this list have the potential to exert some sort of power or control in certain areas of your life. Relationships with the men on this list are not originally intended for romantic intimacy. You have heard the saying, if you don't start any trouble, there won't be any trouble. You really have to count the cost of every decision you make.

Suppose you entered a romantic relationship with your landlord. What is the worst thing that could happen? What if the relationship did not work out? Would he interfere when you started a new relationship with someone else? Would he harass you and hold back the favors or courtesies he once extended to you? What happens to your privacy? He has the keys to your home and can enter at any time. What if he is collecting perks from other female tenants as well? What if he takes a liking to your pre-teen daughter? These are just some things to think about.

It is amazing so many women decide their pastors should be allowed access to their stuff. I caution you with a single pastor and I will call you out for entangling yourself with a married pastor. These men are human and temptation does not exclude them. You could be kicked out of your church; your reputation will be ruined. What would your mother think? Could you tell your grandmother what you have been doing with her pastor? Or better yet, if you are a mother, what lessons are you teaching your daughter? Even if you are not the initiator in this interaction, you will be labeled as the primary villain. By resisting your pastor's improper advances, you also protect him. Shut it down!

Like landlords & pastors, teachers, counselors, doctors, therapists, coaches, and bosses have the ability to affect your life positively or negatively. If these relationships remain professional, you will probably not have any problems. Did you know these positions have ethical codes of conduct and employment laws designed to keep grown-ups from behaving inappropriately? Teachers should not date their students. Doctors and counselors should not date their patients or clients and supervisors should not date there employees or subordinates.

In the workplace interoffice relationships may be classified as sexual harassment depending on how the relationship began, even if the involved participants are co-workers. When this type of thing happens, one person usually has to leave their position; because, it creates a conflict of interest and bars objective management authority. When these relationships go sour and they often do, it costs the company time and money as the participating parties are not able to function at their highest performance ability. If you have met a wonderful man on the job and want the relationship more than anything else, start looking for a new job.

People in teaching and helping professions take pledges to not cause harm to their patients, clients, or students. These types of inappropriate relationships are always harmful to the student, client, or patient. There are laws to help protect you when these professionals lose their capacity to do what is right.

You probably believe you have a certain understanding of the men on this list. Your current understanding of their role may block you from seeing aspects of character not revealed by their titles. Just looking at the list, most would be comfortable assuming these men would be trustworthy, kind, good with children, polite, considerate, etc. It may not be the case. These redeeming qualities may just be a part of the job and not a part of his personal philosophies. Remember, actions reveal beliefs. The men on this list are often mentors and saviors in many ways. They make repairs in our homes, care for us when we are ill, issue our paychecks, and petition to give us raises. You may observe one of them providing loving care for your struggling baseball or football player. Please remember, it is their job to do the things they do and they should do their jobs well. It is not personal; do not get sucked into the fantasy that can easily be created while observing them at work. Also, there are tons of other women thinking the same things about them. Keep it in perspective.

THE OFF LIMITS MEN LIST

Do NOT give YOUR STUFF to your Landlord.
Do NOT give YOUR STUFF to your Pastor.
Do NOT give YOUR STUFF to your Doctor.
Do NOT give YOUR STUFF to your Teacher or Professor.
Do NOT give YOUR STUFF to your child's Teacher or Coach.
Do NOT give YOUR STUFF to your neighbor's man.
Do NOT give YOUR STUFF to your boss at work.
Do NOT give YOUR STUFF to a co-worker in your immediate department.

Do you remember Porsche and her William? He was Tim's awesome coach. He could also fit in this list. Do you see how it turned out for her? Porsche was in position to observe William's acts of service. His roles and behaviors as a coach did not accurately reflect how he would behave in other relationships. I know you have heard of these types of situations before. You either know of someone who has been involved in these types of relationships or you know someone personally. If you have watched only a few TV programs, you have seen it all.

Lucia's Story

Fifteen years ago, Lucia was at the top of her game. She was a young, beautiful, and sassy single lady. She had a body that made every man and woman stop and stare, even if just for one moment. During this time, she was employed as nurse's assistant, with the middle school in her hometown. It wasn't long before the principal began to express an interest in her. Sean pursued her constantly without reservations. Initially, it was easy to deny his advances and requests for dates, she had standards, but, as time passed it became a little more challenging to resist his proposals. After all he was the principal, in addition to being smart, he was also quite handsome. A vacancy announcement for a Bilingual Counselor Assistant position was posted and Lucia decided to apply. This position would increase her pay and her status; she had a high school diploma but she had not been to college. She did it, she put in the application and Sean immediately pulled her paper work. Without delay, he scheduled an interview with Lucia, the assistant principal and himself right after school. We know this was not the correct protocol; needless to say, she was offered the position and she accepted.

The propositions continued; after the promotion, denying Sean a simple date after he had so graciously offered her the position, seemed wrong. She gave in and the adventure of dating such a prestigious and generous man became overwhelmingly captivating. He took her on lavish tropical vacations and theater and celebrity events as he wined and dined her. He would spare no expense to make her happy and he bought her expensive jewelry and clothes. Before she knew it, Lucia was in love. He gained access to all of her stuff.

After two years of the most memorable courtship, she was confronted by co-workers and administrative staff members at the school, who questioned her inappropriate relationship with their principal. She was given an ultimatum to resign from her job and relocate to another school within the district or they would terminate her without pay. Lucia hired a lawyer because she felt she was being wronged, the administration suspended her for three weeks with pay. Her co-workers began to isolate her and treat her as if she wore a scarlet letter on her chest. Sean was not married, he was also single; but, you would not have known it by the way they treated her. She was embarrassed, angry, and ashamed and she did not know what to do. A conversation she had with Sean determined the next course of action. He was the principal, he had been in his position longer, he earned a greater income; she would have to make the sacrifice and leave her position and the school. Reluctantly, she relocated to another school while he maintained his job.

Through-out this entire ordeal, Sean was never questioned or disciplined in any way for his inappropriate relationship with Lucia. Technically, he is the person in the equation who violated policy and employer ethical standards; she was the subordinate. This would have been a classic case of sexual harassment, if she had not grown to love him, which caused her to also protect him. Why was he granted immunity? Why is there inequity between the sexes? Although the ultimatum was placed on the table for both Lucia and Sean, it was obvious the target was Lucia. Her notable work ethic and tenure did not matter. She knew her educational background and work experience could not measure up to his, but this knowledge does not remove the sadness and pain of being treated like the violator, instead of the victim she truly was. She begrudgingly resigned and was disturbed by this ordeal for a long time. Lucia's scenario ended better than many others, she got her man, Sean asked her to marry him and she accepted. Even so, the experience of their beginning is a difficult subject for her to speak about, till this day.

Jennifer's Pain
Jennifer was a cute, witty, young mother who was putting herself through college while holding down a full time job. She was independent and self-sufficient and did not depend on her parents to bail her out of anything. She managed her resources and was determined to make a better life for herself and her daughter. Jennifer was 30 years old and her daughter Madison was 13. Jennifer was recently promoted on her job and received a nice increase in pay, and she also just received a large income tax return. It was time to shop. With the extra funds, she decided it was also a good time to move. She did some research and found an attractive and clean two bedroom apartment, in a newly built apartment community, conveniently located within walking distance to the Metro station. She applied, was accepted, and moved in.

The seasons changed from Spring to Summer and now Fall. One afternoon, Jennifer happened to run into her property manager, at the mailbox and he struck up a conversation that was different than their previous conversations. Devin was new to the community management team and had been in his position for about three months; he transferred in form another property. On another occasion she ran into him at the gym in the community center and he asked her for a date. As demanding as her schedule was, the date did not happen right away but eventually they did go out. He was a nice likeable guy. One date lead to another and soon they became an item, and he began to visit frequently and even stay the night. Madison liked him too; sometimes he would help her with homework. When he stayed the night, he was supposed to leave in the morning before Madison awoke, so she would not know he had spent the night in her mother's bedroom.

As they began to spend more time together, Jennifer discovered a few personality challenges and habits that weren't so likeable. She was head strong with opinions about everything, he didn't like that. Oops did she smell alcohol on his breath after he came to her home late one night? And what's that smell, is that weed? She really did not want this type of influence around her daughter but there it was, and she invited it in. She did not end the relationship but when she was not pleased with his habits, she would put him out of her bed room and he would spend the rest of the night on her sofa. When Devin began to feel Jennifer pulling away, he became jealous and possessive and would accuse her of seeing other men. He began to retrieve her mail and let himself into her apartment during the day when she wasn't home. She wasn't seeing anyone else, her course work became more demanding and she had to spend more time on campus in the library and with study groups. Madison was independent and could take care of herself until Jennifer came home. Jennifer had classes two nights a week after work.

One evening when Jennifer had classes, Devin became frustrated when he was unable to contact her and went to her home. He let himself in and discovered Madison was in the shower. He helped himself to a drink, put his feet up, and turned on the television. Madison was startled to find him in the apartment when she got out of the shower; she dressed quickly and was uncomfortable with him being there without her mother. They did not talk much, she sat at the table and did her homework and he watched the tube until Jennifer came home. The tone of the evening lightened up when Jennifer arrived. Devin told her he had just arrived minutes before she did. As tired as she was, she cooked dinner and they all ate together. Madison said goodnight and went off to bed. Jennifer and Devin stayed up and watched a program as he rubbed her feet to help her relax. She was tired and drained; it had been a long week. She cleaned up the kitchen and got a shower, while he watched another show. While she was preparing to go to bed, he came into her bedroom. She was not in the mood and he wanted to be with her. They fought and she put him out of her bedroom and he went to the sofa. It wasn't long before the entire house was quite, everyone had fallen asleep. Hours later, he heard Madison get up to go to the bathroom. After she went back to bed, he waited until she was settled and then he went into her bedroom…

This tragedy could happen with any immoral man; however, this property manager/landlord had greater access than the typical man would have. Should Jennifer have allowed him to stay the night or sleep on the sofa in such a short time of knowing him? If he saw Madison only in passing instead of in up-close and personal environments afforded by dinner and homework, this may not have happened to her. He was in position to see her smiles and the twinkle in her eyes, up-close. He was able to see her girlish body begin to transition into a more mature form. Why did this mother assume this arrangement would be safe? Did her past have similar conditions? Jennifer clearly took a risk, which exposed herself and her daughter to a terrible experience that will never be forgotten.

REFLECTIONS

Take a few moments and think about your past relationships with off-limits men. Did a teacher, coach, or your boss compromise his position in an attempt to get your stuff? Consider what you will need to avoid these and potential future off-limits men. Take your journal and answer some important questions about your relationships.

Questions

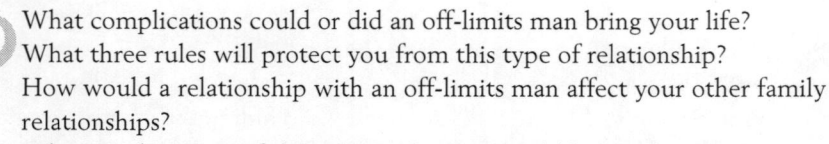

What complications could or did an off-limits man bring your life?
What three rules will protect you from this type of relationship?
How would a relationship with an off-limits man affect your other family relationships?
What are the issues of this relationship you could live without?

Apply the LOAV Method to your off-limits man if applicable.

RRMS. Consider measures you need to have in place to avoid off-limits men. Record at least 3 measures or steps for your personal Relationship Risk Management Strategy (RRMS) regarding off-limits men.

7

Not Ever Men

A violation by a man on the Not-ever Man list creates wounds that may never be completely healed. Some relationships should always be considered sacred and undefiled. It is never appropriate for a family member to become sexually involved with another family member. This is called incest and it destroys individuals and families from the core. Fathers should never have sexual activity with their daughters or their sons. Mothers should never have sexual activity with their sons or their daughters. Brothers and sisters should never have sexual relationships. The same goes for uncles and aunts and cousins. I must now also mention grandparents and step-grandparents. Stepparents should never have sexual relations with any member of the new family. Step-grandparents should never have sexual relations with any female or male person in their family. Being a step-relative does not negate the obligations to protect and support.

Rebecca

I met Rebecca a few years ago. She is bright, intelligent and very attractive but she does not know it. You see, her mother had a few challenges when she was a baby and she was taken from her. Her aunt who was a young wife and mother took her in as her own and formalized it with adoption. Her cousins became her brothers and sisters. When she joined the family, she had an older sister and a brother already in place. Her mom had another child a few years later. When Rebecca was in the fifth grade, her step-father took a special liking to her that was "different." He interacted with her differently and began to have sexual relations with her. This went on for several years before it was discovered and yes it tore the family apart. Her parents are now divorced.

To this day, she has conflicting thoughts and emotions. This man has been in her life since she was a toddler. He is her father and she loves him. But she knows he also harmed her in ways far beyond her ability to express in words. She has forgiven him but the family is still broken, her mother's heart is broken and their family will never be the same again. After a decade has passed, she still wonders if she did anything to cause this to happen to her. Did she make him do it? Did she enjoy any part of it? This is one of the worst things that could happen to a young woman. To this day, she attracts and is attracted to men who do not truly love her. They only reaffirm her feelings of insignificance and disgrace.

For scriptural reference see Leviticus Chapter 20 in the Old Testament of the Bible. The New International Version Bible reads like this:

Leviticus 20:11, 12, 14, 17, 19-21

[11] "If a man has sexual relations with his father's wife, he has dishonored his father. Both the man and the woman are to be put to death; their blood will be on their own heads.

[12] "If a man has sexual relations with his daughter-in-law, both of them are to be put to death. What they have done is a perversion; their blood will be on their own heads.

[14] "If a man marries both a woman and her mother, it is wicked. Both he and they must be burned in the fire, so that no wickedness will be among you.

[17] "If a man marries his sister , the daughter of either his father or his mother, and they have sexual relations, it is a disgrace. They are to be publicly removed from their people. He has dishonored his sister and will be held responsible.

[19] "Do not have sexual relations with the sister of either your mother or your father, for that would dishonor a close relative; both of you would be held responsible."

[20] "If a man has sexual relations with his aunt, he has dishonored his uncle. They will be held responsible; they will die childless.

[21] "If a man marries his brother's wife, it is an act of impurity; he has dishonored his brother. They will be childless.[1]

If this act is by rape or violence the victim is not at fault and will not be found guilty. I just wanted to share this because these inappropriate interactions are specifically addressed a long time ago and they have always been a problem for mankind.

I must tell you when these events occur they create so much shame it is almost unbearable. You probably know someone who has either been molested or taken advantage of by someone in their family or close to their family. There are some women who force female and male children into lewd sexual activity. Men are not the only deviants. Unfortunately the unimaginable may happen and a child is conceived through these crimes. A child conceived through this violation is forced to bear shame.

According to my faith, the only person who can truly help a person deal with this type of shame is Jesus. Many years ago, I worked for the Department of Social

Services in Washington, DC. As a part of my training, we were taught to encourage mothers applying for assistance to provide the name of their children's fathers even if they were not prepared to pursue child support. We were told about delinquent and irresponsible fathers who moved around town. A father could have children in many different areas. For example, he might have a daughter in Northeast and have a son in another part of town.

We were told to get the fathers 'names listed so his name would be remembered by the mother and by the children. If Erica in Northeast met John in Southwest, they would need to know if they were family and if they had the same father or not. If they never heard his name this would be impossible. In the old days, we were taught if these unions brought forth children, the children would automatically be physically deformed or disabled. This thought is partially true. When these unions create children, genetic factors that would predispose them to certain conditions and diseases are doubled. Siblings who share one parent also share some of the same recessive genes. This multiplies a child's disposition to respiratory challenges, circulatory and cardiac conditions, and developmental and learning disabilities, even if the parents do not have these complications.[2] Studies have discovered, children produced by incest have increased chances of having learning disabilities.[3]

We need to teach our young people that romantic intimacy between relatives is never acceptable and never appropriate and that they should immediately seek help if they experience any warning signs of trouble. Troubled signs include feelings of any form of arousal or excitement connected to inappropriate suggestions or environments with relatives. Children need decisive instruction as to how they are supposed to handle this type of situation. Thoughts and feelings alone do not make people good or bad. Their actions determine how their value and contributions will be judged. And yes, we are supposed to judge people. I am tired of hearing we are not supposed to judge one another. How can I help you if I cannot tell you the truth about you? How can you sharpen me if you have grown dull?[4] We are our brother's keepers[5] and this requires rightly judging circumstances,[6] event, and actions. I thank God that we cannot send anyone to hell but we can discern[7] that a particular behavior or action is harmful or simply not productive for the good of all parties concerned.

Ignorance or lack of knowledge never takes away the damage of the scars left behind. Joyce Meyers is an amazing woman of God who shares her testimony of victory over the traumatization of sexual abuse by her father[8]. She is so much more than a survivor. Please check out her books and visit her website. You will be blessed.

I have to tell you it saddens me that a form of this trauma exists in my family. I was not molested by any of my fathers or anyone in my family. However, one of the fathers in my life became romantically involved with one of his cousins when he was a teenager. This cousin had moved in from out of town, and was relatively new to the area. A consensual act or encounter between relatives does not justify or make it acceptable. This is an example where boundaries must be formalized and adhered to. Through their union a child came into the world.

I was never told about my brother until I was an adult. My father bore this shame without any release. My father committed suicide, in the same year I told him that I had unexpectedly met my brother, while visiting my mother's hometown. It was also in this year, my father communicated with my brother for the first time in his life. All his life, he never knew who his father was. My brother was robbed in so many ways. Only one person in my father's family will even speak to my brother. Like it or not, he is my brother and their relative also. To be completely honest, I have challenges relating with him even though I acknowledge him and love him. A grown man walked into my world and wants and needs to hold an important role in my life. We are so different. It is difficult to process. Why does my brother have to carry this burden?

Mothers I call you to teacher your daughters about this potential evil. You do not have to instill fear in them; however, they need to know about other types of strangers like family stranger dangers. Certain boundaries should never be compromised. More often young ladies are harmed more by people they know than by total strangers[9]. Assault and molestation most commonly happens by someone who is very close to the family and even more likely an actual family member.[10] Young ladies need to know what to look out for. She needs to know what the signs are and what environments produce inappropriate situations. Before middle school, you have to find a way to educate them in a way you know, they will get it. A good friend of mine said that when her children were toddlers and preschool ages, she made up special code names for their private parts. So they could talk nonchalantly about sensitive things right in front of anyone. No one knew what they were actually talking about. She would ask them, did anyone play with your Mati doll today?

Do not depend on or wait on the school system to teach your children about sex. Your children need to know what you think and believe about sex in a manner that is appropriate to their ages and stages of development. They are your children, take care of them. School systems begin sex education and family classes by middle school. You would be surprised about the information many children have learned while still in elementary school. For many children middle school is too late because many have already become sexually active. Do not wait for someone else to do the job you are supposed to do. Is it easy? No, but it is absolutely mandatory for the health and wellness of our children. There are some things which cannot be undone or unseen so prevention is the best scenario. Prevention is better than cure, prevention is better than a healing, prevention is better than a miracle.

THE NOT EVER MEN LIST

Do NOT give YOUR STUFF to your friend's man, ever.
Do NOT give YOUR STUFF to your sister's man, ever.
Do NOT give YOUR STUFF to your brother's man, ever.
Do NOT give YOUR STUFF to your cousin's man, ever.
Do NOT give YOUR STUFF to your mother's man ever.
Do NOT give YOUR STUFF to your Father, or Uncle, or Brother, or Cousin, ever.
Do NOT give YOUR STUFF to your Grandfather, Grandmother, or any step-parent or relative, ever.
Do NOT give YOUR STUFF to your children's friends, ever.
Do NOT give YOUR STUFF to a man on the Down-Low, ever.

REFLECTIONS

Take a few moments and think about your past relationships. Is part of Rebecca's story your own? Consider what you will need to avoid and protect yourself and your children from not-ever men. Take your journal and answer some important questions about your relationships

Questions

If you have had this type of experience, what steps of forgiveness or help have you taken to start the healing process?

What are three rules you need to make to protect yourself from the men on this list?

What would you tell your daughter or younger self about the truth of this type of tragedy?

The LOAV Method does not apply here!

RRMS. Consider measures you need to have in place to avoid not-ever men. Record at least 3 measures or steps for your personal Relationship Risk Management Strategy (RRMS) regarding not-ever men in your life or family's life.

8

Dangerous Men

I must say, I have been blessed not to have ever been in a relationship with a man who was physically violent with me. Note, not all dangerous men are physically aggressive or violent. I do have a few friends who have had such experiences. Maybe you know someone who has been in an abusive relationship. Some Dangerous men make the men on the other lists look like saints with the ugliness they leave in their wake. A short stent with a Dangerous man can be extremely volatile and damaging. This chapter is not fun or funny in any way. It must be included so please bear with me.

Typically dangerous men are abusive. Abusive characteristics of dangerous men include consistent bouts of anger or angry moods. Dangerous men also have tendencies to be jealous and possessive. Anger may be used to control how you spend your time and not allow you to give much thought to your family connections or other relationships. A possessive man will not care about you spending quality time with your family.

Women who have survived child abuse, battered women, and survivors of rape are often referred to as victims of domestic violence. Abused women suffer from learned helplessness and come to believe they cannot prevent the abuse from happening. The perpetrators of these violent crimes are often physically stronger or excessively controlling. These types of domination, cause abused women to function in a survival mode instead of looking for a path of escape.[1] Ladies, we all need to become aware of the many types and forms of violence and abuse against women.

TYPES OF ABUSE

Relationship Abuse

There are several types of abuse you need to understand. Relationship abuse is a term used in reference to abuse in romantic or intimate relationships.[2] It is identified when a partner in the relationship exhibits, abusive and controlling behavior toward the other partner. Other specific types of abuse may occur within romantic unions include but not limited to sexual, emotional, physical, verbal, and financial.[3]

Non-physical forms of abuse are devastating to a woman's level of daily functioning and her self-esteem. Even just one type of abuse, in a relationship is a clear indication the relationship is not healthy. If you have observed a friend in this type of relationship, you should encourage her to get some help. The victim and couple should get help, whenever possible. The reality is for many women, these are life or death circumstances. A habitual violent situation can easily escalate to a loss of life without much notice at all.

Sexual Abuse

The most common types of relationship abuse are sexual and physical.[4] You cannot be sexually or physically abused and not be emotionally affected. Please know rape is not the only type of sexual abuse acknowledged by the law. Undesirable or unwanted touching, forced decisions about the use of or elimination of birth control, forced pregnancy or abortions, withholding sex, demeaning sex, and sex after a violent event, are all considered sexual abuse. [5]Statistics report between one half and one third of women are raped by their partners. If your boyfriend, man, or husband forces you to have sex, it is considered sexual abuse.[6]

Physical Abuse

We know physical abuse is easier to identify because of the evidence it leaves behind. In addition to hitting, kicking, biting, scratching, choking, it also includes holding a partner captive or preventing them from entering the home. Physical abuse is the only one form of abuse easily punishable by law, because of the physical evidence remaining.

Emotional Abuse

Emotional abuse is the often invisible type of abuse that can be as damaging if not more debilitating than physical abuse. A woman who is constantly criticized, belittled and minimized is being emotionally abused. Emotional injuries are also created in environments which facilitate or endorse controlling, ignoring, or silent treatment behaviors.

Signs of an emotionally abusive relationship are more subtle than physical and sexual abuse. Name calling, jealousy, spying, isolation, and control may not be so obvious to people not familiar with the partners in the relationship.[7] Blaming, threats, over-involvement, and, fear of your partner without reason or cause should not be ignored.

Denial is a common symptom in all forms of abuse. In denial, a woman will refuse to acknowledge she is actually being abused. Sisters, verbal abuse, as intermittent as it might be, leads to other forms of abuse, in many cases.[8] Denial can make it hard to encourage our friends to seek help or get away from their abuser, especially if they move to the next step, which is justification. Justification entails excusing or covering the abuser's words and actions because he was angry.[9] Justification is an indicator the cycle of abuse has gone to the next level. Consequently, by this time abused women usually begin to have physical symptoms as a result of the abuse. Physical symptoms of abuse include stomach aches, tension headaches, ulcers, and panic attacks, etc.[10]

If you suspect you are involved with a dangerous man, you should pay attention to conversations and events and listen for content regarding violent activities, use of drugs, and non-consensual sex. Dangerous men may also have a variety of other challenging addictions. Dangerous men may behave inappropriately with children or may be attracted to children.

You may not have had control over the circumstances of childhood abuse or the initial abusive relationship that created your state of learned helplessness. However, today is a new day, and you can take the steps for your freedom and safety. You can do something about it. Talking with someone you believe you can trust is a great place to start. Other options include seeking a therapist or crisis counselor who can teach you about your human rights and women's rights and what will be needed to effectively plan the end of the abuse and abusive relationship. Counselors can also help locate resources and safe houses to will assist your transition to a more healthy and joyful life.

Grace Got Away

Grace did all the things most young girls are primed to do. She was an excellent student in high school and a creative wizard in college. She had a gift that added life and color to everything she touched. Projects, events, parties, menus, programs, photos paintings came to life with the slightest effort. Grace is an amazing artist. Beneath this gift of creativity was a warm, generous hearted, sensual woman who managed to be shy yet engaging and involved simultaneously. Simply put she was beautiful. It was not possible to look into her mocha brown eyes and not want to be invited into her life or her world. She was told she was beautiful all her life. But, she did not know exactly how beautiful she actually was.

Grace graduated from college and moved back home to Philadelphia. She was able to get a great job at Pennsylvania State and rented her first apartment. Her future looked promising and her family was so proud. Then it happened, she met him. One Fall evening, right after her birthday in November, Grace met, Owen, a super fine smart young ex-football player turned businessman. Owen was like a dream. He was polite and considerate; and did I say fine? He did all the things gentlemen are expected to do. He owned his own home cooked for her and wined and dined her. He would send flowers to her office and take her away on spontaneous trips. Owen made her feel important and adored.

Approaching the one year mark in this fantasy relationship, it was clear she was completely in love with him. At this point several things began to change. Owen became controlling and possessive without cause. He began to ask detailed questions about all of her past relationships. He would take her phone bill to review her call log, to see who she had been talking to. This unfounded spirit of dominance was fueled by uncontrollable anger, jealousy and rage.

Grace had dated a few basketball players in the past and Owen happened to follow the game. If one of her ex-boyfriends was in a particular game, Owen would immediately start slinging the insults about the player and Grace. He would get so angry he would lash out and hit her. If she was not there and he watched a game without her, he would call and threaten her. This is clearly the behavior of a man who is not well. After these outbursts, in person or over the phone, he would plead and beg for forgiveness. He would say thing like, "I can't live without you." "I need you in my life." "I'm no good without you." "I promise to do better." "I've never loved anyone as much as I love you." These professions would be followed by a series of convincing events.

Grace did not know how to handle or end this relationship, therefore, it continued. This cycle of abuse began to break her down and challenge all the good things she thought about herself. Her love began to turn into resentment and regret. What happened? You see, Owen was the youngest of ten and his younger life was always difficult and strife filled. He watched his alcoholic father beat his mother. Money was tight and everyone had to work. Owen had also experienced inappropriate touching by a near relative. Owen was even beaten by his father even as an adult. There was a lot of hurt in his life. He knew of a God but he did not personally know God or any form of spiritual truth. He was angry with a lot of people about many things. In fact, he was a miracle. His level of accomplishment and success were not typical of individuals with his experiences. On the outside and on paper he appeared to be the perfect guy. Unfortunately pain induced ugliness was alive inside of him. He felt cheated and entitled and he took this out on Grace.

Grace finally realized as the incidents progressed, her life was in danger. During her initial attempts to end the relationship, she left her home and went to stay with friends in an attempt to elude or lose him. While she was away, Owen convinced her landlord he was her husband. The landlord gave him a set of keys to her apartment. One afternoon she stopped in to get more clothes to take to her friend's house, only to discover he had been there. Broken glasses and dishes smashed against the walls lay in wake of his visit. When she had the locks changed, he then pursued her on the job. When she went to the police for help, they told her they could not do anything until he put his hands on her. Well, he had already done that...

At some point Owen began to back off and she found out he decided to get some counseling. Thank God! He invited her to join him but she declined the invitation. She knew she would surely need psychiatric care if she remained in this relationship. Grace was now fully aware of the dangers of her situation and knew she had to do something serious and drastic to remove herself from this dangerous man. She packed up and moved out of state and started a new life, a much more cautious life. Seven years later he tracked her down and apologized for all the ugly things he had done to her. He was still single, never married, and without children. This is probably a good thing. Grace did what grace does. She has found a way to forgive him; but, she knows she will never be with him again and she will never forget. Grace got away!

How did Grace miss all of these issues? What did she see in plain sight? What did she choose to ignore? What undisclosed events of her past allowed her to endure this relationship? (What was her relationship with her father like? What were her expectations? What did her relationship models look like?) Is there any level of abuse that should be tolerated or excused? NO!

THE DANGEROUS MEN LIST

Do NOT give YOUR STUFF to an angry man.

Do NOT give YOUR STUFF to a jealous or possessive man.

Do NOT give YOUR STUFF to a man who wants to control you.

Do NOT give YOUR STUFF to a man who stops you from spending time with family.

Do NOT give YOUR STUFF to a man who stops you from going to church or growing in your spirituality.

Do NOT give YOUR STUFF to a man who behaves inappropriately in front of children or is attracted to children.

Do NOT give YOUR STUFF to a racist man.

Do NOT give YOUR STUFF to a man who is dishonest.

Do NOT give YOUR STUFF to a man who is violent.

DO NOT give YOUR STUFF to a man who hits you or curses you.

Do NOT give YOUR STUFF to who is always drunk.

Do NOT give YOUR STUFF to a man who is addicted to drugs, sex, or pornography. (Or any other known addiction.)

Do NOT give YOUR STUFF to a man who is untrusting of everyone.

Do NOT give YOUR STUFF to a confused or unstable man.

Do NOT give YOUR STUFF to a man who is involved in relationships with other men.

Do NOT give YOUR STUFF to a man who wants to be a woman.

Do NOT give YOUR STUFF to a woman who wants to be a man.

Do NOT give YOUR STUFF to a man who wants you to give your stuff to his friends.

Do NOT give YOUR STUFF to a man who does not respect women.

Do NOT give YOUR STUFF to a man who does not respect authority.

Do NOT give YOUR STUFF to a man for money.

Do NOT give YOUR STUFF to a man who makes you feel bad about your stuff.

Do NOT give YOUR STUFF to a man who is unwilling to meet your emotional needs

REFLECTIONS

Take a few moments and think about your past relationships with a dangerous man. Do you have an Owen in your history? Consider what you will need to avoid these and potential future dangerous men. Take your journal and answer some important questions about your relationships.

Questions

What unaddressed issues allowed you to enter a relationship with a dangerous man?

What are the types and signs of abuse?

What three rules will protect you from this type of relationship?

What are the issues of this relationship you could live without?

Apply the LOAV Method to your dangerous relationships if applicable.

RRMS. Consider measures you need to have in place to avoid dangerous men Record at least 3 measures or steps for your personal Relationship Risk Management Strategy (RRMS) regarding Dangerous men.

9

Toxic Friendships

Ladies we often give ourselves away in non-romantic circumstances as well. We have been known to give ourselves a way to jobs, causes, and events which become more important than our health and more important than our families. This is a problem. A major point of surrendering your stuff also happens with girlfriends.

We give our stuff away to friends who are not true. These so-called friends do not have your best interest before them and actually may have intentions to harm you. You need to be in a position that allows you to observe all people you are planning to invite into your inner circle or inner world. It is very important not to establish relationships or fellowships with people who lack integrity. As in romantic encounters, the signs are there if you pay attention.

We often talk about relationships between men and women and expect these relationships to have some ups and downs in communication. Partners in romantic relationships are aware of the possibility of the union working out and the couple staying together or not. The potential for either option is always present. Many years ago, most married people did not think divorce was an option. Today people get hitched with the assumption and consideration of knowing, if doesn't work out for them according to their plans and desires, they can get a divorce. Unfortunately, a formally acknowledged protocol for ending same sex friendships or breaking up with girlfriends has not been drafted. Relationships with mean girls are potentially as damaging as relationships with dangerous and unavailable men.

Tanisha

A young lady named Tanisha shared a painful experience with me. She went out with a few young ladies she thought were her friends. Tanisha was a college student who was an inexperienced drinker. Her friends were able to convince her to sample a few drinks. When she became drunk as they knew she would, they left her in the company of a man she barely knew. This man forced her into sexual activities while she was intoxicated. Clearly these ladies were not her friends. The signs these girls were not her real friends had been ignored or excused for some reason or another.

When people do not treat you well, you don't have to take it. You don't have to be friends with people just because you are class mates or members of the same groups or even your church. Real friends will look out for you.

Jezzie

Naomi had a friend named Jezzie. I say had because they are no longer friends. Jezzie was an imposture friend. When Naomi and Jezzie met, Naomi was already married. It was interesting, the next few gentlemen Jezzie dated all had a resemblance to Marcus, at least Jezzie thought so. On two separate occasions Jezzie reported to Naomi her dates "look just like your husband just like Marcus." Naomi did not think anything about it.

Jezzie went on to date other men and decided to make Marcus her dating advisor. She would call for his advice. So in essence she began a relationship with Marcus that did not include Naomi. She would call when Naomi was not at home. Jezzie even began to question Marcus about some details of his marriage. Her flirtation with Marcus continued in a subtle manner. When she would visit, she would make sure she wore form fitting clothes and showed just enough cleavage.

One of Naomi's sisters was coming into town and she shared this information with Jezzie. There was a good possibility the two would have an opportunity to meet. Jezzie began to ask Naomi questions about her sister and about what she looked like. Naomi replied, her sister is absolutely beautiful. Well wouldn't you know it, Jezzie did get a chance to meet Naomi's sister Rachael. One of the first things she said with a negative tone was, "Oh, Naomi said you were beautiful." She then turned to Marcus and said, "Marcus, what do you think, is she beautiful?" For the record Rachael is a beautiful woman. Marcus is a good man and he had the right response. He said she looks just like Naomi, they are sisters. Marcus told Naomi she needed to fix her friend. What kind of mess was that? Oh I forgot to mention, this Jezzie is also an Ordained Minister.

Somehow, this event was overlooked and the friendship continued. Jezzie had an opportunity to visit Rachael's home while on a speaking tour, in New Orleans. She took time to meet with and get to know Rachael's children, while she was there. It was also reported she thought it was appropriate to share her negative sexual experiences with them. Imagine that. Humph!

Hold on, it gets even more interesting. Naomi invited Jezzie and her mother over for a holiday dinner. Naomi's children and her relatives would also be there. Before Jezzie arrived, she had started on a bottle of wine and she brought another one with her. She was feeling pretty good when she arrived. Mind you, no one else at Naomi and Marcus's home drank alcohol so Jezzie and her mother would be enjoying this bottle of wine by themselves.

After dinner, desserts, and a lot of warm fellowship, Ms. Jezzie begins to tell a story about two dogs in heat and what they do when they are in heat. She got on her hands and knees lifted her leg to the side and began to physically gyrate, acted out the motions, and imitated the sounds of a dog in heat, leading up to and including the sounds of "completion." All of this took place on the family room floor in front of everyone. In addition to other family members, Naomi and Marcus's daughter and sons were also present.

When Naomi demanded that Jezzie stop this inappropriate activity, Jezzie responds by saying, "I know yawl still do it!" At this point, Naomi could no longer excuse or ignore Jezzie's behavior. The signs of Jezzie being a toxic friend were present right from the beginning. Jezzie thought she was untouchable and she was always in the middle of an act of division, between friends, siblings, and co-workers. She behaved as if she was the most "beautifulest" of them all. Well, her mirror, mirror on the wall lied to her, because her insides were not pretty at all. Needless to say this 20 year toxic relationship came to an abrupt end. It existed for far too long.

Okay, let us break it down. Ladies be wary of a woman who constantly compares her man to yours or is preoccupied with your man in any way. Your friends should never have access to private conversations with your man. This could have gone in a completely different direction. Marcus just happens to be a good man. A toxic friend may flirt with your boyfriend in inappropriate ways in front of you or interact with your brother in other indecent ways. When you learn a so called friend is having inappropriate conversations with your children, or behaving inappropriately with anyone in your family, you need to shut it down fast. Do not tolerate this type of contemptuous spirit.

If you personally have not experienced a toxic female friend, you know someone who has. Toxic relationships may also be revealed by the negative influences your friend has on you. The not so respectful things you find yourself doing when in her company, i.e. addictive behaviors, smoking, excessive drinking, drugs, gossiping, promiscuity, and being mean to others. If she doesn't tell you the truth when you need to hear it, she will lie to you without skipping a beat. This so-called friend may have established a habit or cycle of disingenuously flattering you, putting you down, and thoughtlessly telling your secrets.

Friends at Work

When you go to a workplace everyone should not be granted immediate access and entrance to your circle; everyone will not be your friend. Do not tell your personal business to everyone. You have been placed there for a reason and there are no coincidences or accidents. Despite the circumstances and what you may have heard, you get to judge and decide who will be close to you. You do not get to pick your parents or siblings; but you do get to pick your friends and associates. You will be associated with the good your friends do and all the ugliness they create. Would you want to be known by her reputation? If a relationship with a female friend constantly has you feeling anxious, worried, threatened, or in trouble, you need to evaluate the relationship. Ask yourself what level of stress does this relationship bring into your life? What does this person offer you in the relationship?

When a true friendship is balanced it operates more like a partnership with concerned and committed investors. Balanced relationships provide give and take in partnership and fellowship. Both parties come to a meeting together and both of you should have something to offer one another. Exchange is not always momentarily balanced. At times your friend may have more to offer you than you have to offer her. This is acceptable as long as the tables turn. Other times may require you to be more of a rock for her. What do you have in common? What are her goals and philosophy on life and spiritual beliefs? Are they compatible to yours? You need to know these things. It is not about the number of friends you have but about the quality of friendships you have.

Do you cry?
Yes, we all cry at some point, some of us cry more than others. While watching movies with my daughter I often hear, "Here come the water works." I'm easy; it doesn't take much to get me going. Now in life I don't cry a lot but when something really hurts I don't hold back. If you are not with me in those moments you will not see it. Even though I don't cry a lot, I do not hide my feelings and I will meet the challenge of conflict with a friend before I run from it. If you run from it, you will only have more to deal with later. I have been repeatedly accused of being too happy or smiling too much. How could someone be that happy all the time? Well, fake is one thing I have never been. When you get me you get the real me. Crying or not crying does not make you stronger or weaker. Crying is the result of emotional expressions and we all process and express our emotions very differently. Crying is not always an indication of a true sign of remorse or pain. Some people cry when they are actually happy! If a friend needs to see you cry or witness you being vulnerable or feeling pain for any reason, there is a problem. If she is truly a friend and has been with you, she should have been able to observe these things at some point in your relationship. You will not cry, hurt or rejoice in the ways she does and she should not require you to. You are your own person. If you find your friend telling you to do you differently, she doesn't really get you. You might have to work on your relationship a little more or reconsider if the friendship is one you should keep.

Saying Goodbye
One of the best ways to end these types of relationships is to simply end it. Stop the loss. Depending on her personality you may have the conversation in person and explain your differences as you would when ending a romantic relationship. Chances are you will run into her at some point in the future. It would be good to simply inform her, you will not be able to embrace her the way you once did. This will diffuse any awkward future public meeting. Expect some sort of back lash or rebuttal but you need to hold your ground if you have made a decision based on solid data supported by continual negative experiences with her.

If you can, return her belongings and cut the ties. You do not have to be nasty or vindictive; just be a real woman and pray for peace, healing, and development. BUT, just like in some romantic relationships which have gone sour, civility may not be an option for you. You know who you are dealing with and what you will need for separation and closure. Make it happen soon rather than later.

Today, I watched an episode of Katie's Take on Yahoo. The episode title was *How to Survive a Friend Break-up*. Katie Couric was interviewing Counselor and Author Dr. Irene Levine about her new book titled, *Friends for Life: Surviving a Breakup with your Best Friend*.[1] Dr. Levine explains, there are two primary reasons friendships end. One reason is people grow apart as a natural course of life. People change. The other reason friendships end, she referred to as "big betrayals" or "friendship killers."[2] I enjoyed and agreed with her statement that friendships need to be nurtured and or pruned regularly and social media is not a substitute for friendship.[3]

I have had to end a few relationships because I realized the relationships were more damaging than good. For most of those break-ups I had the conversations. I have also been rightly dropped by a few friends because I was misbehaving…that attraction to unavailable men got me in trouble with a few friends. There are some things I would do differently, if given the opportunity. And I would like to apologize to every friend I have disrespected or hurt because of my iniquity, selfishness, and immaturity. Neither side of the breaking-up process feels good, the dropping side or the being dropped. We know when we have made huge mistakes and when it is our fault something has ended. Be honest, apologize and choose a graceful exit when you can.

When you breakup with a friend, you should be honest and cautious not to intentionally damage your friend's or former friend's self-esteem or play a blame game. It is usually never about the actions of just one person. Dr. Levine says, "Friends are more important than family in conferring longevity; people with an extensive network of good friends outlive those with fewest friends by 22%."[4] You can access Dr. Levine's blog on www.theFriendshipblog.com for more information.

Jesus had a posse of about seventy men.[5] Of the 70, only twelve[6] had esteemed positions. Out of the top twelve were three.[7] What does it look like for you? Who are your top three and why?

One More Thing

It's about your money. Money conflicts are among the common challenges which often ruin friendships and relationships. It has a lot to do with your personal beliefs and relationship with money. I happen to manage my money relationship by budgeting, sacrificing, and a little planning. Last year I came across a book that is sure to set you on the right path. I will refer you to an expert: Wealth Coach, Deborah Owens. Mrs. Owens is the author of *A Purse of Your Own: An Easy Guide to Financial Security*. You can read her blog and contact her through www.deborahowens.com. She can help you create a "Purseonal Financial Success

Plan." To get a head start, make a list of your monthly expenses, detail information about your credit cards, loans, and any other debt, get a free copy of your consumer credit report at www.annualcreditreport.com, and identify your net income, what you bring home after taxes and insurance, and all sources of income. Once you have located and gathered this information, you are ready to do the work. If you have financial troubles, you will need to develop a healthy relationship with money and create a prosperity definition, which is holistic and not only focused on financial gain.

THE TOXIC FRIENDSHIP LIST

Do NOT give YOUR STUFF to a "friend" who is selfish.
Do NOT give YOUR STUFF to a "friend" who is jealous of you.
Do NOT give YOUR STUFF to a "friend" who lies to you.
Do NOT give YOUR STUFF to a "friend" who tells your secrets.
Do NOT give YOUR STUFF to a "friend" who makes advances on your boyfriend or husband.
Do NOT give YOUR STUFF to a "friend" who has slept with your boyfriend or husband.
Do NOT give YOUR STUFF to a "friend" who will not look out for you.
Do NOT give YOUR STUFF to a "friend" who flirts with you father.
Do NOT give YOUR STUFF to a "friend" who interferes with any of your other relationships.
Do NOT give YOUR STUFF to a "friend" who behaves inappropriately with your siblings or your children
Do NOT give YOUR STUFF to a "friend" who borrows your clothes and returns them soiled or torn without compensation or apology.
Do NOT give YOUR STUFF to a "friend" who always wants you to pay when you go out together.
Do NOT give YOUR STUFF to a "friend" who clearly is a gossiper and untrustworthy.
Do NOT give YOUR STUFF to a "friend" who encourages you to behave inappropriately or to participate in unhealthy or illicit activities.
Do NOT give YOUR STUFF to a "friend" you cannot trust.

REFLECTIONS

Take a few moments and think about your past friendships. Is there a Jezzie or friends like Tanisha's friends in your past or present?

Questions

Who are your closest friends and why?
Do you have some friendships you need to reassess?
Why did you originally allow her to be in your world?
What can you do to establish healthy boundaries for a potentially toxic friendship?
What are the qualities of true friendship and what compatibilities do you require?
What would you tell your daughter or younger self to warn or protect them from the individuals you have encountered on the lists, we have discussed?

Apply the LOAV Method to your most important friendships. What patterns have your discovered?

RRMS. Consider measures you need to have in place to avoid toxic friendships. Record at least 3 measures or steps for your personal Relationship Risk Management Strategy (RRMS) regarding Toxic women folk.

PART II

10

Attachment Styles

*"Love is our true destiny.
We do not find the meaning of love by ourselves,
we find it within others."*

~Thomas Merton

I am not sure of what you have heard about Attachment Styles but the theories provide insight to our preposterous human condition. Dr. John Bolby has been credited with the development of the Attachment Theory in counseling[1]. Bolby explains attachment as a "lasting psychological connectedness between human beings."[2] The core premise of the attachment theory revolves around mothers of infants and their accessibility and responsiveness to their child's needs. Mothers who are willing, available, and sympathetic to their child's needs create a sense of security within the child.[3] This sense of security allows a child to explore his or her environment and feel safe.

I am not planning to bore you with psychological shop talk, so give me a moment. Just note, what we learned as children is what we still do as adults when it comes to established patterns of behavior.[4] How we attached molds what we believe about who we are and how were interact with other. I found the attachment theory more interesting when it was presented by Dr. Tim Clinton and Dr. Gary Sisby. Clinton and Sisby co-wrote a book called *Attachments*. What drew me in was the subtitle: *Why you Love, Feel and Act the way you do.*[5] In this book you learn Attachment styles reveal the learned patterns of dealing with presented and potential dangers are physically manifested or in the mind. Attachment styles are constructed from early childhood and are reinforced by repetitive events and life experiences.[6]

Women who view themselves unworthy of love or do not trust others to provide the love they need will often replace the need of love with unhealthy communication, material gains, work, drugs, sex, and other addictive practices Understanding the formation of preferences, habits, and past experiences enables people to make changes to improve current and future relationship outcomes.

To see where you are in this area, you need to answer two core questions:
"Am I worthy of love? And am I capable of getting the love I need?"[7]

You see, how we live and the choices we make in all areas of our lives are directly connected to our core beliefs. Our core beliefs about ourselves and our beliefs about others we are in a relationship with, will dictate our decisions. What we believe about ourselves is learned from interacting with those around us. From my study of attachments, I learned early experiences and interactions with our original and primary caretakers provided messages told us we were loved, beautiful, special, smart, capable, and important. Unfortunately, some of us received messages which were the complete opposite of acceptance and sufficiency.

Other negative messages many received were that they were not important, not beautiful, not smart, not loved, not special not capable or worthy of anything. A woman who had loving positive parental relationships would conclude she did have value and the world might be a strange and interesting place was safe to explore. Secure or loved women trust others, take chances, and contribute in relationships because it was modeled for them. They are taught their emotions can be managed and others are available to support them in times of need, discomfort, or sadness.

Those of us who did not have this loving and secure base often resist being open and sharing in relationships and do not trust others easily. The tendency to be untrusting is a learned practice. Parents who failed to adequately love, protect, and provide for their daughters produced women who find it difficult to trust others.

Injuries sustained by non-secure women or people in general are called soul wounds. Soul wounds can occur at any age; however, soul wounds are most severe and damaging in the early years, because young children lack the experience in cognitive processing to properly assign responsibility for their hurtful or traumatic experiences. With this limited knowledge and lack of understanding, children make decisions which go unchanged from childhood to adulthood.

Now that you have thought about the core questions, here are two more to help you dig a little deeper. Your answers to these questions not only reveal your beliefs about self but also our beliefs about others. These additional questions include: **Are others capable of loving me? And are others accessible and willing to respond to me when I need them?**[8]

In chapter three, I spoke about the iniquity challenges passed to me from previous generations. I did not talk about the good things my mother did give me. I know for sure, I was unconditionally loved by the entire family she bought me home to. She was my Mama and her Mama was my Mama too. I had two mamas and several relative papas. I was securely attached in my early years and was conditioned to fight or press for what I wanted. She didn't allow me to be sick (unless I really was). I couldn't use common excuses to get out of things. She convinced me; I could do whatever I set my mind to do and she had great expectations for me. I watched her take classes or lessons in roller skating, macramé, stain glass, modeling, and photography. She even learned how to make the Cabbage

Patch Dolls when they first came out. She was creative and industrious like her own mother. She did not recognize how gifted she was; but this did not keep her from passing those good things on to me and my sisters. My mother is a great and generous lover of life and I am proud of her and her personal growth. Because of her and my GrandMary, I knew I was truly loved and I was capable of getting all the love I needed plus more. I may not have had the most productive romantic relationships but I knew who I was and I was never confused about where I ended and my partner began.

Remember our strongest emotional expressions are tied to our closest relationships and our core beliefs. This is why giving our stuff away is not limited to any group regardless of sex, age, race, education level, social status, or income. These core beliefs directly affect your ability to form healthy boundaries. A woman with non-secure attachment does not have healthy boundaries and in relationships, she has difficulties determining where she ends and her partner begins. This makes it easy for her to begin to give her stuff away without being fully aware of what she is doing. If you have not had healthy relationships modeled for you by someone who also demonstrates positive core beliefs, you will find it difficult to imagine what it could feel like.

REFLECTIONS

Take a few moments and answer the questions for yourself.

Questions

Are you worthy of love? Why do you believe you are worthy?
Are you capable of getting the love you need?
How do you know you are capable of getting the love you need?
Do you know what unconditional love feels like? If so, describe it.

11

Relationship Boundaries

If you do not control your mind, someone else will.
~John Allston

When we hear the word boundary, we are inclined to think of gates, partitions, and geographical borders of countries, neighborhoods, school zones, sporting events, etc. Boundaries usually surround and protect items of value while blocking adversarial entities or circumstances which would bring harm to the valued possessions. On farms, boundaries keep domestic animals in a safe environment and predators on the outside. Concepts of borders and boundaries are predominately about property ownership and maintenance of our stuff. We place great value on manicured fenced yards and gated communities. Therefore, a boundary is synonymous for safeguard, protection, and preservation. Do you leave expensive jewelry, financial documentation, or money on your living room coffee table when you are hosting an event at your home? No you put them away for safekeeping and you are selective with whom you will share them.

Well, guess what? You are your most valued and prized possession. I am going to keep telling you until I know you know it. You are your best tangible and intangible asset. And there is only one of you. You are an exquisite and rare being. There is not another person on this expansive world like you. If you have never thought of yourself as a valued possession and the ultimate prize, chances are you have not established healthy boundaries for your relationships. Attachment styles and boundaries are interconnected. In relationships, the dominant boundaries are emotional and physical; they determine how you will interact, touch others, and receive touch.[1] How you give and receive touch and manage your emotions is molded by your attachment pattern. Emotional boundaries determine our emotional expressions and feelings in connection with others. Physical boundaries specify proximity comforts or prescribed personal space, for in person or face to face interaction with others.

Your healthy boundaries will be firm yet flexible and they will help you protect and maintain your unique qualities.[2] Boundaries are supported by active and functioning concepts which allow you to maintain independence and connectivity in relationships simultaneously. Stringent boundaries may provide protection in unfamiliar circumstances and frightening events.[3] Relaxed boundaries promote intimacy when safety and trust are established. If you have healthy boundaries you know how and when to say no to any request that does not present options which are good for you.[4] Boundaries also protect your needs and encourage self-respect.

A woman who has healthy boundaries has a strong sense of identity and has a solid knowledge base of self-understanding. She can clearly express her own needs, desires and feelings in a relationship.[5] Women who have healthy boundaries are accountable and responsible for their own actions and consider their needs as important as others. Women with healthy boundaries will not auction off their integrity or reputation for frivolous reasons. More importantly than many items discussed, a woman with healthy boundaries understands she is the only person who is responsible for her happiness. It is her assignment to learn how to keep the balance and address and adjust her expectations of herself and others. No one completes you like you.

A woman who does not have healthy boundaries finds it difficult to say no when asked to add one more thing to an already hectic schedule. She is afraid of rejection and will go to great lengths to avoid it. Unfortunately, she will constantly experience victimizing circumstances because she gives over her self-control liability to other people all the time. The problem is systemic and not limited to romantic relationships.

Women with unhealthy boundaries define themselves by other people's thoughts, desires, and projections and not their natural gifting and aspiration. They easily give of their time, money, spirit, and body. Think about the women you meet on the way to work. A woman with unhealthy boundaries may be identified as the stranger who sits next to you on the train and shares very personal and private information because you smiled and shared a kind word. She may also "fall" in love easily as she interprets friendly conversation and attention for more. This woman may have been severely emotionally and or physically wounded. She may be trying to keep life together for everyone but for herself. Ladies, you are not responsible for other people's processes and happiness. Take this off your to do list. Do not compromise your values and ideas because of small challenges or resistance to avoid rejection or conflict.

Some women have very rigid boundaries. This too is unhealthy.[6] Women with rigid boundaries have very little trust for others and they have mastered the art of shutting people out. She is the co-worker who is nonchalant and distant. She does not share feelings or show any emotion and has an air of being completely self-sufficient. She does not need anyone for anything. Rigid boundaries will keep other people away emotionally and physically. You could put a sign on her saying access denied because she will not allow anyone in.

If you realize your gates and boundaries could use a little tweaking or a complete makeover, be encouraged, you can create healthy boundaries and change your life whenever you make the choice. It may feel strange or uncomfortable in the beginning because your current habits are attached to deep rooted childhood experiences and early attachments. If you feel a little anxious or scared, note the feelings are normal and part of the healing process. Just remember, it will take some time but you will be able to make a successful transition if you commit to a *practice for change*. Sheer willpower will not be enough. You will have to put thoughts and plans into actions. Establishing goals that can be charted and measured produce the greatest change results. These goals should be achievable and allow you to take one step at a time. How did you get here in the first place? Let us examine what is needed to begin to create and maintain healthy boundaries.

Note on Touching
Touching or the lack of touching is a significant element in the creation of attachment styles and boundaries. When you touch someone or receive touch from someone many things are happing. There is no such thing as a simple touch. Touch creates and or embellishes chemical, emotional, and spiritual bonds.[7] Every touch has a motivation and a purpose. A mother's touch is different from a pat from a teammate. A lover's touch is different from a touch from a friend, at least it should be. We touch people we care about and sometimes we touch people we do not care about. Sometimes our touches hurt the people we care about. Like our spoken words, our touches should be thoughtful, intentional, and for a purpose. We often begin to surrender our stuff with what appears to be a simple act of touching. Decide that you will only give and receive touch with clear purpose and motive.

Creating Healthy Boundaries
We can agree poor boundaries are the consequences of low self-esteem which often originates from insecure attachments, false and irrational thoughts, negative emotions, and self-destructive actions. These conditions cause beautiful and valuable people to give themselves away.[8] After acknowledging that we are challenged in this area we can take steps to reverse the curse.

How do we start?
We start with forgiveness (fer-giv-nis). That's right; you can say it, **f-o-r-g-i-v-e-n-e-s-s**. Forgiveness is a process that enables and facilitates your heart's movements toward emotional and psychological healing and freedom. With forgiveness, you will learn how to give yourself permission to release injury and blame, to heal emotional wounds and move beyond pain and memories of past events. Walking out on a forgiveness process allows you to detach from dead memories, it reframes your past, and paves the way for the establishment of new or improved healthy boundaries, for you and for others in your life. As you prepare to create healthier boundaries your journal will become one of your best tools and favorite retreats.

You can begin the next activity now or when you have completed the entire book. It is the core of the healing process that will allow you to set up a better home security system for your stuff. Forgiveness is not about excusing the terrible things someone has done to you. It does not replace justice. Forgiveness is not about turning the other cheek or pretending you are not hurt or angry because it is the Christian thing to do. Forgiveness is about reclaiming your power and not allowing the person who harmed you or the hurtful memories to dictate your future. Forgiveness is about giving more of you to God and allowing him to teach you about his kind of love. Your identity is not found in the sum total of all the bad things that happened to you. I highly recommend beginning your Personal Forgiveness Project (PFP) as soon as possible. Today is always the best day to start something new.

YOUR PERSONAL FORGIVENESS PROJECT

Part I

1. First, take a few days to spend time researching you. Observe your daily interactions and record your feelings, thoughts, and actions.
2. Next, analyze the data you have gathered and identify the issues and participants. It would be good to enter this step over the weekend. While you are becoming more acquainted with your stuff, make or purchase an attractive keepsake box to place your valued stuff in. Decorate it and personalize it. Think of it as a treasure chest designed to hold your most precious jewels, diamonds, rubies' sapphires…
3. Make a list of your observations designating the discoveries as positive or challenging. List the people who caused or triggered challenging memories or experiences. Positive observations will report actions, thoughts and events that reveal your current perceived value, and levels of self-respect and self-care and compassion for others. Challenging observations demonstrate anxiety and fear associated with interaction or passed events, feelings of extensive obligation and insignificance.
4. Once you have identified these unhealthy expressions record the specific details of their triggers and how they present. When you have completed this step, take a break and do something special for yourself. It is likely you will feel emotionally exhausted as you remember or relive negative memories.
5. Create a list of affirmations expressing your desired behavior responses to apply like healing ointment to cover these memories or triggers when they surface. I do not believe there are negative affirmations; they are just lies. For this project, an affirmation is a positive declaration of truth about you, your experiences, your people and your stuff. They will not include any negative or past tense words. Instead, affirmations are statements infused with positive descriptive truths about your present and future state of being, conditions, and

achievements. Think of it as painting a picture of the life you desire by creating it with your words. For example, "I don't lose my temper as much as I used to," sounds like a positive statement; however, if you examine the words you will feel some resistance. Positive affirmations will include expressions without resistance. Examples:

I am achieving greater control of my emotional responses every day.

I am smart and beautiful and in control of my life.

My family loves me and we are growing in understanding and acceptance of one another.

I am worthy of love.

I am forgiven.

Good things pursue me every day[9].

I am blessed and highly favored.[10]

Record as many affirmations as you like; but, do not create less than seven. Repeat them in the morning before beginning your day and in the evening before your retire. During one of these times, say them while looking into a mirror.

6. Practice saying no and stop trying to be Miss Fix It, all the time.
Start this practice now. Say NO out loud right now. Okay, NO. Say it again. NO. Say it one more time and change your inflection. NO. How did that feel?

Part II

With this preliminary work done, you are now ready to enter a more advanced stage of your Personal Forgiveness Project.

1. Make a list of everything you are grateful for in this world. Write as long as you have to. There isn't anything too silly to be grateful for so don't hold back. Start each statement with, "I am grateful for…"

2. Again, list the people you identified as contributors in your hurtful memories. As terrible as these people may have been to you, can you remember anything good about them? If so, write the good things down. Ask God to help you forgive them.

This may sound crazy; however, I would like you to ask God what he would give you if you forgave the people on this list. Yes, you are thinking, "No way, you can't do that. You can't make a deal or bargain with God." Well one of my dearest friends who is also one of the sweetest and most giving woman I know shared she had a un-forgiveness issue. I never would have thought it. While in a counseling session with a Christian counselor, the counselor asked Angela this question, and her eyes and mouth opened wide just like yours did when you read the statement. The counselor insisted she ask the question and she did. God responded and gave her a personalized gift in the form of deliverance that can never be taken from her. It changed her life and softened her heart. So, don't put God in a box, don't decide what he will and will not do. He is a parent and parents will do almost anything to get through to their children.

The question the counselor presented is supported by scripture. Psalm 15:2 states "The one whose walk is blameless, who does what is righteous, who speaks the truth from their heart." And Psalm 84:11, "For the Lord God is a sun and shield; the Lord bestows favor and honor; no good thing does he withhold from those whose walk is blameless." Angela was seeking assistance with a condition of acknowledged un-forgiveness; it was an incredibly heavy burden. God knew who hurt her and what her struggles were. He knew her heart wanted to do the right thing. Angela made a choice, to walk upright before the Lord in forgiveness and he exchanged the ashes of her burdens and depression and gave her the beauty of freedom and peace.[11] The good news is the Holy Spirit will take hold of those of us who have been brokenhearted and wounded, to free us from the darkness of un-forgiveness and pain, exchanging his beauty and freedom of love for our ashes.[12]

3. Write a letter in your journal to the people you have selected for forgiveness and share with them why you have chosen to forgive them. Then write a letter to yourself explaining you have forgiven yourself and why.

4. Identify and record any positive thing that may have resulted from the negative events.

5. Create seven new self-love affirmations for yourself and write them down in your journal. The content of these statements should include new affirmations regarding your greatness, new boundaries, and new positive self-discoveries. Don't worry if you are not feeling everything you are affirming. Affirmations do not always produce good or positive feeling immediately. It may take a little time but don't skip them just because you are not feeling them. The truths will eventually become more evident as you continue the work.

6. Take your first seven statements and write them on small strips of paper. You will create seven new entries each week for four weeks. That's only one a day. Record them in your journal an on small strips of paper and place them in your valuable Stuff Management Treasure Box. This box will hold all your good, reclaimed, and new stuff. Once your box is full it will be a place to go for your own personalized inspiration and motivation. You are the prophet of your own life, speak it.

Throughout your forgiveness process make sure you appreciate your needs are as equally important as other people's needs. Make a decision to not live by allowing others to define you. The word no is not always a token of rejection. Many times it simply means not now. Saying no more often will also make it a litter easier to take when you hear it. No is not an automatic personal rejection. There is a time and place for every condition in our lives.[13] You may have to tell yourself, no means not now and not always never. You may feel a little selfish in the beginning but most people will learn to accept your boundaries. Expect your new boundaries to be tested by those close to you and also be prepared to meet the real you.

To start toning your boundary muscles examine your daily schedule and reserve at least a half hour of "me" time every day and protect this time. As you have discovered, a significant part of boundary setting involves self-love, self-respect, and a practice of forgiveness. Setting boundaries is not about playing games or playing hard to get. Do not use boundaries as excuses to play hooky or skip out on your daily obligations and responsibilities. Boundaries entail making the best decisions to protect your most valuable commodity and asset, YOU. Be intentional.

LIFE GOALS

Since we have covered attachment styles and boundaries and you have started or begun your PFP you are now in position to take a more aggressive stance toward some of your original goals and dreams and to make new ones. You now have a better understanding of why you have done the things you have done and can begin to take corrective measures to do the thing you want to do. Boundaries will help protect your goals and plans for your future, goals you want to accomplish and dreams you want to live.

When you were a little girl, what did you want to be when you grew up and why? Are you working in the field of your choice today? If you are not doing what you wanted to do why aren't you? Do you still have the same desire or dreams today? What could you do to get back on track?

If you are a young woman, have you made plans to finish college before starting your career and starting a family? Have you ever written these plans down? Take some time to seriously think about your life plans and write them down. After you have recorded them establish markers that will allow you to see your progression toward specific goals. For example, if one of your goals requires additional education, look into a few schools and find out what the admission requirements are. There are many grants and programs in place to assist you with picking a new career or transitioning into a new one.

If you want to own your own home examine your debt to income ratios and create a plan. Financial planners can help you with this for a minimal fee and you can get free information on line. If you would like to complete college and gain experience before starting a family you have to have a plan. If you don't make your plans visual and tangible it is not likely they will come to pass. I know this from personal experience. What you do not want to happen or even imagine is often what happens, when you do not have a real plan.

Do you see how boundaries and managing your stuff could help with this plan? If you do not have a plan and have not set boundaries to help protect your stuff, what defense would you have against a fun, strong, good looking man who happens to be described in one of the lists? Plan ahead, maintain healthy boundaries, grow in the knowledge of your value, and protect your stuff. Take out a big beautiful calendar and start plotting your future, one thought, one action, and one goal at a time.

PART III

12

Managing Stress & Emotions

Have you ever felt as though your multiple roles and responsibilities were physically resting on your shoulders? Are you sandwiched between caring for your children and simultaneously taking care of your parents, while still meeting the demands of full-time employment? Or, are you a full-time student who has to also put in full-time hours on a job to pay for school? Are you a new wife and a new mother? All of these scenarios can be overwhelming and notably stressful. When so many people and activities compete for your time and energy, it is easy to keep sacrificing your own needs and pushing them farther down your list of priorities. You feel forced to abandon your good intentions to exercise more, plan healthier meals, read a good book, or work on the crafts you once loved. Business as usual and stress of life have robbed you.

What is Stress?
The condition of being "stressed" has physical, emotional and eventually psychological implications. Stress and emotional distress are tightly interwoven agents and the manner in which a woman deals with stress is directly connected to her ability to manage her emotions. If you can manage your emotions you will be more equipped to manage your stress.

Stress is a protective mechanism initiated by the body and it may be defined as an event or situation an individual perceives to be physically, psychologically or spiritually dangerous.[1] It may also be defined as the effects: thoughts, emotions and behavior brought on by the perceived threat. Our ability to handle stress is not so much about addressing the issues presented to us, but rather how we deal with them. Many things can create or contribute to a stressed state including a poor diet, lack of physical activity, inadequate sleep, chemical substances, work challenges, romantic conflicts and negative thoughts. Negative thoughts top the list.

We must understand, stress is not something that arbitrarily or randomly happens to us. We have the ability to exert influence and choice over the presentation of stress in our lives. Our health is greatly impacted by our abilities to handle stress. A condition of chronic stress can have a serious impact on our physical and spiritual wellbeing. Sustained high levels of the adrenaline released in the body produce a 'fight or flight' response.[2] In a crisis, internal adjustments are made within our body to prepare us to act in self-defense for self-preservation.

Stress related illnesses include heart problems: high blood pressure, heart failure, heart attacks; susceptibility to infections: allergies, autoimmune diseases; skin problems: acne, psoriasis, eczema and unexplained rashes, pain, muscular pain, headaches, herniated discs, fibromyalgia, repetitive strain injury, back, shoulder and neck aches, diabetes, and possibly infertility.[3] This list is way too long for something that can be controlled. Health professionals are certain; stress suppresses the immune system creating a target and vulnerability for infections. Women who tend to be impatient, excessively competitive and hostile run a higher risk of heart problems due to long term reactions of stress.[4] Get your emotions and thoughts in check. Don't be a hot head. It is not cute and it doesn't make you "strong". High blood pressure also known as hypertension is a common chronic disease and it usually does not have any obvious symptoms. Even so, it raises the risk of stroke, heart failure, kidney failure and heart attack. Heart disease is said to be the number one killer of women.[5] In women heart attacks often begin as mild symptoms as a slow building pain. We are so used to working through pain and doing whatever we have to do to take care of our families; the signs are often ignored. You should partner with your doctor to determine your risk levels for heart disease. A happy heart plan can save your life and save your family from the heartbreak of losing you prematurely.

Stress may also affect your appetite, elimination, sexuality, and sleeping habits. Significant weight loss or gain in a short period of time may be a symptom of depression resulting from continual stressful conditions.[6] Difficulty sleeping may be one of the first noticed signs of stress. The average person needs to get seven to eight hours of sleep daily in order to meet the body's requirements for rest and repair.[7]

True stress management is not about avoiding stress but, rather, learning to manage or control its recurring effects. Effective stress management requires a personal commitment to schedule the required time and effort to study your emotional responses and habits and to learn stress managing skills. It is our perception of stressful circumstances that determines the magnitude and type of emotional and physical arousal we experience. If you are experiencing frequent negative moods this is a sign stress is having a negative effect on you. Negative moods are often magnified when the feeling is the focus and not the cause of the problem or situation.[8] If you are serious about learning to manage your stress and emotions, you will also need to examine your sleep, exercise, nutrition balance, and relaxation habits.

Sleep

Let's get back to the sleep issue. Sleep is one of the most important tools to establish or maintain health and wellness.[9] Sleep does the body good. Inadequate sleep is known to be a contributing factor to obesity and hormonal disruptions.[10] When you are in deep sleep your growth hormones are released and they, boost muscle mass and repair the tissues and cells.[11] You also learn better, respond faster, and feel better when you are well rested.[12]

Exercise

Exercise is another wonderful resource to assist in the management of stress and related issues. It happens to provide what is referred to as positive stressors. Adequate and proper exercise functions as a tune-up to your whole body. Exercise assists in the creation of stronger internal balance structure.

Daily movement, increases your energy levels, fights chronic degenerative diseases, enhances your mood and helps with weight loss or management. [13], Women who exercise properly on a regular basis are generally, happier, healthier, and stronger.[14] They also report having more satisfying sex lives than women who do not exercise. Even though exercise requires energy, over time it significantly increases your energy resources. Think of it like money. You have to spend a little to make it and the more you spend if you do it wisely the more you make.

Nutrition

I am sure you ready know nutrition is another area extremely important for health New dietary suggestions are displayed by a plate and is divided into four sections being fruits, vegetables, grains, proteins and a side of dairy.[15] We are encouraged to monitor our portions and calories and increase our intake of fruits and vegetables, whole grains, and water. Use caution with foods that contains high sodium content often added to soups, breads and processed foods and frozen meals.[16] You can check it out for yourself at www.ChooseMyPlate.gov. Like Mama always said, Eat your vegetables."

Balance

Balance is about scheduling effective relaxation. Relaxation is a journey and not a final destination. The first step on this journey is learning to become aware of what puts us out of balance and when. The next step is to choose and practice steps that will return us to balance when the events of life disrupts our peace. [17]Balance between home and work life is a challenge for most women and even greater challenge when you are responsible for other people and have multiple roles. You need to consider scheduling regular salon and spa treatments or massage to help you relax and balance the demands of your life.

Relaxation

Relaxation is the foundation upon which all the other stress management techniques are built. It is where restoration and balance begin. Most of us know what is needed to take better care of ourselves but we do not do it. We believe we are giving and nurturing when it comes to taking care of others. However, there is a part of us that knows we cannot really love others until we have learned to love and accept ourselves.

So, how can we really care for others if we completely neglect ourselves or at least parts of ourselves? Are we giving our best or some generic brand of care, love, or assistance? Remember what the airline hosts say? They always instruct mothers to put on their oxygen masks first. If you cannot breathe what good are you to anyone else? Taking time out to take care of yourself is like a proactive first aid treatment for the health of your family. If you really love then and want the best for them you MUST do it. You must take care of yourself; it is not selfish.

Simple Stress Reducing Strategies

We have already established that journaling is a wonderful way to get in touch with your feeling and experiences and begin to make sense of things which did not make sense before. You can use your journal to determine your priorities and look for solutions. With this purpose a journal can show you when you need to share responsibility. I hope you are enjoying your journaling in your current process.

Delegate and renegotiate deadlines. One of the most important skills we can ever learn is an effective way to manage our stress. Delegating is a great tool to help manage stress at home. Effective stress management requires our personal commitment to schedule the required time and effort to learn the stress managing skills.[18]

Often those around you won't realize how overloaded you're feeling. Manage your time wisely and prepare for events as much as possible in advance, without becoming a perfectionist or expecting others to be. When you experience severe physical and emotional symptoms, seek professional advice. By being in tune with your emotions and knowing your stressors when you're under stress, you can take action as soon as possible.

We all know solutions are easier said than done, but, they are worth every effort. There are times when you must take a "me first" attitude. Throughout time and in different religions, our bodies have often been referred to as temples. A temple is a sacred and cherished place that contains and protects priceless substances.[19] A temple is a place of nurturing, honor, and respect which cultivates, balance, peace, and hope. So you might be thinking, where do we start or how do we start this restoration process? We must start with some form of a plan.

Stress Managing Practices

I have listed a few stress managing practices you can actually start using today. You do not need to go anywhere or purchase anything. You may have to close a door and find a comfortable place to perch or lie but you and your intention are all that is needed to start these activities right now.

Deep Breathing

Breathing is absolutely everything. It's the beginning of us when we are born and the end of us when we pass on. Without food we can live for about four weeks.[20] Without water we can live up to 14 days[21]; and without oxygen we can only live for three to five minutes depending on the environmental circumstances.[22] This tells just how important breathing is. Without oxygen, the brain cells are the first to go after about four minutes.[23] Loss of consciousness happens between eight and ten seconds after oxygen rich blood supply to the brain has stopped.[24] The brain only makes up two percent of our body mass but it uses 20 percent of the oxygen we take in.[25] Naturally it makes sense; breathing is one of the first things we can do to address stressful conditions.

When we are stressed, our breathing is usually flat, short, and labored. Our breath goes into our upper chest or shoulders. This type of breathing increases tension. Deep breathing or diaphragmatic breathing requires us to breathe with our bellies.[26] If you have every observed a sleeping baby, you noticed the gentle rise and fall of their bellies as they inhale and exhale.

When we consciously engage in deep breathing we shift our focus to an internal focus while deflating external concerns and events. We become calmer and think more rationally. Deep breathing is a technique that allows you to acknowledge the moment and shift stressful thoughts of the near or far future into a non-threatening category. Breathing deeply, inhaling from your abdomen instead of your chest, provides more oxygen to your bloodstream and can help you control your emotions and stay calm.[27] To start, place your hands over your belly and slowly breathe in through your nose. Feel your stomach expand, and then slowly exhale. If you can fit this simple exercise in each day for an initial 10 minutes you will find you experience life much calmer with greater control of your stressors and emotions.

Meditation

Meditation is another way to calm your body and mind by focusing your attention on one thing, such as a phrase, scripture, concept, or positive thought. I do not suggest meditations that call you to empty your mind of all thought. The most common way of meditating is to pick a word or phrase you can say to yourself in coordination with your breathing. If you use a single word, repeat it when exhaling. If you are using a few words, try coordinating some of the words on the in breath and some on the out breath. Combining meditation with conscious deep breathing will provide all the benefits of deep breathing infused with intention and positive affirmations. It is an excellent tool to reframe or reprogram negative thoughts and beliefs about ourselves and our worlds. 10 to 20 minutes a day is all you need to start.

Imagery

If you can picture the tide and the sea shells on the seashore the way they looked the last time you were there, you can practice imagery. Imagery is simply creating a mental picture or scene that can help soothe and relax you. Remembering colors, temperatures and smells will take you there in the memory of your mind. Scenic landscapes, a face of a loved one, picturing positive romantic memories are great imagery options.

Mindfulness

So far, all of these practices are mindful in nature. Mindfulness is simply focusing on the present moment, concentrating on the here-and-now.[28] As you go to or from work, notice your surroundings, appreciate the look of the sky or the sound of a bird. While at work or at home, try to focus on the task or project at hand, without thinking about what you have to do in the next hour or next day. Take pleasure in simple things, like savoring a good meal or laughing with your family and friends. Try not to get distracted by what happened yesterday or what may happen tomorrow. Enjoy today.

The Ultimate Goal: Self-Management

Self-management or self-care is the key to successfully managing stress and emotions.[29] Self-care is the service we perform for ourselves that will produce more energy, more satisfaction, and provide a positive alternative to negative events and feelings. Self-care requires us to take a daily preventative approach and action in the care of our bodies. Relaxation is an essential underpinning of a healthy lifestyle. Women who have the ability to create and choose a "relaxation response" find they become more responsive and less reactive to strssful situations.

Just Think About It, Pick Something and DO IT!

Manicure and Pedicure	Spa	Painting
Massage	Exercising	Listening to Music
Facials	Reading	Singing
Reflexology	Dancing	Making Music
Yoga	Fencing	Reading
Book Club	Sports	Martial Arts
Support Groups	Drawing	

One of my favorite places to untie my body is by taking a Bikram Yoga class. Bikram's beginning yoga class is a twenty-six posture series performed in temperatures similar to a sauna; it is simply an excellent resource for reducing stress. The heat it allows students to warm and stretch muscles, ligaments and tendons, in the order in which they should be stretched. It is a mentally relaxing, internal stimulating practice that gently places the body into correct alignment, promotes greater flexibility and joint functions, while also strengthening and toning the muscles. In addition to the release of toxins and increased flexibility, Bikram yoga offers wonderful benefits for internal systems and organs. Instructors often detail the parts of the body being impacted by particular postures. If you are in Maryland, please visit Bikram Yoga Columbia (BYC), in Columbia, MD www.bikramyogacolumbia.com. BYC also offers massage therapy, skincare services and a host of other wellness and community opportunities. If you are in the Baltimore area, visit Bikram Yoga Baltimore, www.bikramyogabaltimore.com, with about three locations. For me, Bikram Yoga is a gift I give to myself.

If you are in search of natural and organic skincare products, Origins in Columbia Mall is a great location. Origins' online address is www.origins.com. You can pick up excellent skincare products and receive a customized complimentary mini facial with your purchase. Because facial are healing and relaxing, they can easily be included as a regular activity in your stress management plan. Origins carries a skincare line formulated by Dr. Andrew Weil; the system produces amazing results for ethnics, all skin types, and conditions.

13

Prayer

One of the easiest and most effective forms of stress management and stuff management is prayer. It will not cost you anything and it can be done absolutely anywhere at any time. Prayer does not require any advanced degrees or any fancy preparations. It only requires your heart, your mind, your lips or internal voice, and your intention to communicate your concerns, needs, fears, and or frustrations with the wonderful Counselor. There is not a right or wrong way to pray; just find your way and do it regularly.

My prayer life is all over the place, physically and figuratively. There is not a place or time in which I have ever been uncomfortable praying. Unfortunately, many people save prayer for the last resort, for help, when in fact it should be the first. Prayer is not only about you talking to God, it involves your listening. It is not about you limiting your prayers to closed eyes and positions on your knees. Prayer should become an integral part of your daily functioning. Prayer is about your conversations and interactions with God. Prayer is about talking to God like you would talk to your best friend, telling him things you would never tell anyone else even though he already knows. God wants to hear from you. He wants to be involved in celebrating with him your joys and pains. You can share when you feel disappointed or even angry with him. In prayer, you can ask him to give you a hug when you need one. You can crawl up into The Father's lap and feel his breath on your face as he looks into your eyes. Prayer is about dancing with God and inviting him in on everything and every area of life. Passionate prayer often transitions into praise and worship.

A Special Visit
Let me share with you one of my most memorable prayer experiences. One afternoon I invited my Abba Father to come sit with me in my living room. I was toiling with the idea of a potential relationship I knew would not have met my needs or standards. Aspects of this potential relationship were simply amazing while other areas fell short. On this particular afternoon, Father came into my home and

to my living room. He sat on my hunter green oversized micro-suede pillow-back sofa and I sat in an oversized chair adjacent to him. He took up the whole sofa with his magnificent and massive presence. I felt small, honored and surprised. I knew I invited him; however, I was astonished he actually came so quickly. He attentively leaned toward me and we began to talk about this potential relationship. To sum it up for you, he told me it was not about him controlling me. It was not about him blocking certain experiences and expressions from my life.

It was not about me not being allowed to express all of the aspects of myself as a woman. It was not about me not being allowed to be sexually active. It was about his great love and how much he truly loves me and wants to take care of me, all of me. He cherishes me and he honors every piece of me. He would not do anything to harm any part of me. He wants to take care of every need I could ever think of or desire. He allowed me to feel what true honor feels like because he honored me. Can you imagine that? He explained this potential relationship does not and would not adequately honor and cherish me.

You see, I am his baby girl and he loves me crazy and does not want to see me injured or to experience the type of relationship trauma he could see in the future of this connection. He wants me to have the best for me. He wants me to have a relationship with a man who can take care of my emotional needs, a man who can take care of my heart. If a man cannot take care of your heart then he will not be able to genuinely love and honor you. If he cannot take care of your heart he will inflict more harm than good.

After this conversation I felt like something broke inside of me. I felt like my heart cracked or it melted or that something happened within the core of me and all I could think of was a literal OMG! My father loves me so much. How can I honor him? How can I show him I really get it this time and offer my love in return?

This conversation gave me the power to resist the invitation of this potential relationship that would have eventually called me into casual sexual activities and challenged the way I felt about myself. My prayer conversation allowed me to say no, without any further resistance or hesitation. This visit revealed more of my true value and how I should love myself. At the end of the day, physical pleasures without real love are not worth our time or the degradation they ultimately create. Ladies, sex alone will not open the door to a man's emotional heart and it is definitely not the key to our hearts. Sex is not love and love is not sex.

Here is the thought; first of all I want a blessed and honored relationship and marriage. So, a man who wants this role in my life will have to prove he is able and willing to take care of my heart. If the man can take care of my heart, then I know he will have the ability to take care of the rest of my stuff. If he cannot take care of my heart and my emotional needs, then he may not have any of my stuff. The choice and decision to honor myself became simplified.

After this renewed understanding, the internal conflict that would occasionally pull my core in opposing directions subsided, the fight was over. The light bulb went off and I thought this is how I can honor my father, by choosing relationships from his perspective. By choosing relationships from characteristics he would consider redeeming. And then I thought about the scripture when Jesus says, "If you love me you will keep my commands."[1]

Through this experience, I was learning to obey his will through his love for me and not the law. The law could not have convinced me not to get involved in the relationship or not to share my stuff. It would have actually driven me straight to that thing. Because my attention was turned to love, love is what I focused on. And focusing on love and being in conversation with Love enabled me to show my Father love, by honoring what he wanted for me. He wanted me to honor myself. People only do to you what you allow them to do. We consciously or unconsciously grant permission and or participate in the process.

This also took me to another scripture, Matthew 11:30, "For my yoke is easy and my burden is light."[2] Honoring God's will for me in this area and at this moment was no longer difficult. It became easy because of the law of love and not the law of commandments. I learned when you focus on Love all things come into alignment. Have you ever danced with God? Have you ever climbed into his lap to allow him to hold and comfort you?

Prayer Delivers

I made it through a debilitating heart-break with Grayson because of prayer. In that season, I learned to pray like I never prayed before. If you have truly connected with me through my stories you have realized several things. Growing in my knowledge and knowing of God helped me make better decisions over time but I still made and make mistakes and sometimes big ones. The difference is, no matter how good I am or the bad that may come by me, I always know who my Father is. None of my good can save me and none of my bad will make him stop loving me. Truly knowing God and walking with him makes us better but it does not make us perfect. We have to know and internalize his truly unconditional agape (love).[3] It is not based on any feelings or lofty concepts. It is based on his truth and his promises and not on anything we could do or say. Our will power cannot make it happen.

I began to understand God's love for me at an early age. You see, my first name is Princess and this name was given to me at birth. Being my parents' first child and my maternal grandmother's first grandchild, I had the better of two worlds. I was the youngest and the oldest child simultaneously and I could do no wrong. I have been teased about my name most of my life. Most of the teasing has been positive. But this is what I say, A Princess is a Princess and it doesn't matter if she is good or if she is bad. She is a Princess and will always be the daughter of the King. All girls, ladies, and women are Princesses, we are all Princesses. There is nothing in this world that could take us from our positions as the King's daughters.

The prodigal son took his inheritance and squandered it.[4] When he returned, his father had been on the horizon as part of his daily ritual, hoping and waiting for him. On the day the son returned, his father saw him far away and ran to him. When the father reached his son he embraced him with love; [5]the father's love never ended. When the son was out in the world he was still his father's child. That would never change. True, while he was away, he did not reap the benefits of being his father's child or the provision of being in his father's home, but the fact remained he was and would always be his father's son. It was his father's blood that ran through his veins. Likewise, the essence of my Heavenly Father resides within me.[6]

A friend of mine read part of my story and referred to my religious exploration as a season or a condition of a backslidden state. I had heard this term before but never thought of it in application to me. Even if I would entertain the concept, Scripture tells us Jesus is married to the backslider.[7] I found two definitions for backslider. Definition one: to relapse into bad habits, sinful behavior, or undesirable activities.[8] Definition two: to revert to a worse condition.[9]

I was not conscious of an intentional move to become sinful. Yes, I was a bit rebellious, challenged what I was told and explored other religions. The truth is, it was all a part of my search for him; I was still chasing God. In good and bad relationships, I was looking for him and his love. The Word of God says he knows our beginning from our end,[10] and he knows our hearts[11]. When I sincerely gave my heart to Jesus at the age of 13, I believe it was done.

Yes, I went out like the prodigal son. Even while I was away, there were times I would secretly call on him in emergencies. I guess we all know he is within range of our voices; even non-believers are conditioned to call on the name of the Lord when in trouble. Anyway, he always had my back. I left him but he never left me and he never stopped looking for me to return home. Everything that happened after that point is all a part of my journey and my process. It has all been good for me.

On my journey, I practiced non-Christian religions during different seasons of my life. I have also been a member of several Christian denominations. I have been a member of my current church for 12 years and a part of a local congregation for eight. The most important thing I learned in my studies and experiences is the beauty of love is not found in rules, laws, ordinances, and restrictions. The beauty of love as an active force of life is found in people and relationships. Rules and laws are designed to protect us but not to rule over us. Nor are these rules to become our gods or to be used as clever ways to further segregate believers.

If you truly know Love, there is nothing that can separate you from him.[12] My experiences have made me who I am today and I am grateful. I happen to really like me. He continues to show and tell me how much he likes me too. A few weeks ago, I visited a Home Goods store. I saw this framed oil painting that read:

You are the Peanut to my Butter,
Twinkle in my eye,
Blue in my Sky
Shake to my Bake
Glaze to my Donut
Sprinkle on my Sunday
Jewel in my Crown
Milk to my Shake
Flip to my Flop
Sweet in my Dreams
Spring in my Step
Beat of my Heart

I thought how wildly amazing it would be to have someone feel and say those words to me because they earnestly felt that way. I felt a small quiet voice inside saying, "I AM saying these words to you." I began to skip throughout the store like a little girl. I felt as if I were about to float away and I could feel the presence of God right there with me. I began to get this tingling sensation going up and down the left side of my body and around my head. It feels as if I am under water and bubbles and waves are rushing pass me.

This is what I call one of my God Moments. When a God moment happens you know you have been visited by His presence. He is always with us but sometime He shows up in very special ways. Look for your own God Moments or God Sightings. I am so grateful he has chosen me.[13]

REFLECTIONS

Take a few moments and answer the questions for yourself.

Questions

What are you grateful for in this very moment?
What is the one thing you have been praying for a long time?
Do you truly believe God loves you? Why or Why not?
What would have to happen to make you know his love for sure?
What does spiritual forgiveness mean to you? What could you do to revamp your prayer life or your relationship with God and what are you willing to do today?

14

Health & Wellness

True health is negotiated on a cellular level. We are walking and talking conglomerations of energetic cell clusters that form our organs, systems, and physical characteristics.[1] Each cell has a particular tribal loyalty and geographical boundaries. Eye cells cannot function as cells that form your feet.[2] Lug cells cannot aid bladder operations. Each cell in our bodies requires nutrition to function and to live out its life span.[3]

The life of a cell is approximately 90 days.[4] Essentially on a cellular level, you become a new person every 90 days[5]. As the Program Director for Integrative Medicine at the University of Arizona, Dr. Andrew Weil has changed how the world views the aging process. Cells may be educated and trained to function more or less effectively and lifestyle and dietary choices affect your cells and the quality of your life.[6] Your health is a significant part of your stuff that also needs to be managed and maintained.

Numbers you Need to Know

Like wine we grow more valuable with each passing year. As we mature we need to make sure our environments can support the increasing value of our treasure. This responsibility of safe keeping requires us to become more acquainted with our personal and specific numbers. Knowing our numbers is not about obsession but the knowledge will help keep our bodies from crisis circumstances. I am sure you want to know what I am talking about. The top three numbers you need to know in relation to you your health are your blood pressure, cholesterol, and fasting and post meal blood sugar level. Others numbers that may have significance to your personal situation are vitamin D levels and thyroid hormone levels. There are many others but let us start with these. So far, all numbers mentioned are related to the health of your heart.

Blood Pressure

Blood pressure is simply the rate of pressure in which your heart forces blood through your arteries. In a blood pressure reading, the top number is the systolic pressure, it measures when your heart beats.[7] The bottom number is the diastolic pressure and it measures the rests between heart beats.[8] The consensus is the lower the blood pressure, the better. High blood pressure is also referred to as hypertension.[9] If left unchecked, hypertension can lead to heart disease, kidney problems, impaired vision, and even stroke.[10]

Healthy numbers will be 120/80 or less.[11] If you diastolic number is between 80 and 89 and our systolic number is between 120 and 139, the risk factors for hypertension may increase[12]. Knowing your blood pressure reading is not limited to any age group as hypertension is experienced by the young and the mature alike. If you find you have reached the danger zone talk to your doctor and start implementing new practices immediately.

Hypertension responds positively and quickly to a healthy diet low in sodium and fat[13]. It is also reduced by exercise, learning to manage your stress levels, and letting go of the alcohol and cigarettes. Checking your blood pressure is a mandatory step in most physician visits; however, if you are concerned, you can check your own between visits at most local pharmacies.

Cholesterol Numbers:
Cholesterol is not a bad thing. It is a natural occurring fatty substance produced by the body, involved in many important operations. Cholesterol is found in cells, tissues, and organs throughout the body. It may not do what the brain or heart does though we could not live without it. The problem occurs when we have too much low-density lipoprotein (LDL). LDL's are transported by the blood stream[14]. It is responsible for the formation of plaque that builds up and restricts arteries.[15] This buildup of plaque narrows the space for blood flow in the arteries and reduces the amount of oxygenated blood to the heart causing coronary heart disease.[16]

The Ideal level for LDL is less than 100 mg/dl[17] *(milligrams/deciliter)*. You are in the borderline range if your level is between 130 and 159, any measure over 160 is considered high.[18] High LDL levels increase your risk for a heart attack. The good cholesterol is high-density lipoproteins (HDL). HDL works to transport excess cholesterol out of the blood stream and to your liver for proper processing.[19] If your HDL levels are less than 40/mg your body is challenged with an insufficient cleanup crew.[20] The average levels are between 40 and 59 mg/dl.[21] The ideal level of HDL for adequate protection is around 60 mg/dl22.[23]

Fasting and Post Meal Blood Sugar Levels
The healthy range for blood sugar levels range between 70 to 99 mg/dL before a meal[24]. Fasting blood glucose tests are usually performed to screen for diabetes. If levels fall between 100 to 125 mg/dL range it is considered a pre-diabetes condition. Numbers over 126 mg/dL are an indication of official diabetes diagnosis. The results of post meal testing may be more implicating. *Healthy post meal glucose levels are anything less than 140 mg/dL*.[25] If you are in a pre-diabetic state your sugar levels will be excessively elevated after a meal. Readings between 140 and 200 mg/dL are also considered a form of pre-diabetes.[26]

Why do you need to be concerned about high sugar levels? It is really about your heart. You see a condition of high sugar levels may be a viable predictor of heart disease. It seems to all go back to your heart health. If your glucose levels are high after meals even though they stabilize a few hours later, you may still experience damage to blood vessels. This damage can lead to artery plaques and become a contributing factor, in advancing heart disease. It is a big deal. Type 1 Diabetes is a diagnosis usually applied to children and young adults. In the condition of Type I, the body does not produce enough insulin. Type 1 diabetics patients can learn to manage their condition and be happy.[27] Type 2 Diabetics are typically diagnosed as adults.[28] When adults receive this diagnosis it is because their bodies do not produce enough insulin or the produced levels are not detected. In many instances medication is necessary to address this condition; however, there have been very positive reports on healthy lifestyle changes have been proven to be highly effective.[29]

Again healthy lifestyle changes or habits include healthy meal planning, exercise, adequate rest, stress management. You have all heard it before. But you have to know commitment and consistence are the key factors. This is not an area to play around with. You can do the research. When diabetes becomes complicated, patients lose limbs, sight, and many other functions are often taken for granted.[30] I am not sure I believe all the information presented about the groups of people most at risk for this and similar negative health conditions. I do not believe there are truly an adequate number of people of many ethnic groups who see doctors or have tests to make solid conclusions many studies claim. This is part of your stuff so take care of it. Take care of your stuff regardless of what your hear or don't hear about

Vitamin D Levels

Not too many people have dangerously elevated Vitamin D levels. Vitamin D deficiency is more common. Because of my sun allergy, I stay out of the sun and cover up even for exposure as short as 15 minutes. I even burn through thin summer clothing. Because of this and a few other factors, at one time, I had very low vitamin D levels. **Healthy Vitamin D levels are between 30 and 50 Nano moles per liter (nmol/L)**[31]. Just for the record, any levels of vitamin D above 125 nmol/L are in the excessively unhealthy zone. As you can see the complete range is wide due to many varying factors.[32]

Any reading below 30 is considered a deficiency[33] and my level was a 7! Low D levels put you at risk for osteoporosis, hypertension, autoimmune disorders, psoriasis, inability to affectively process calcium, reduced immune function, cancer, and mood disorders[34]. It can mimic signs of depression so make sure your doctor does several tests before he or she decides to hand out the antidepressants. I am pretty sure it affected my mood.

My nutritionist placed me on a high potency vitamin D3 supplement by Life Extension with 5000 iu. I took one capsule twice a day and in three months my levels were up to 32 which my doctor considered healthy for me.

Thyroid Numbers

Generally there are two conditions associated with a troubled thyroid gland. Your thyroid could be underactive creating a condition called Hypothyroidism[35] or over active causing hyperthyroidism.

Hyperthyroidism is a condition in which your thyroid produces too much hormone.[36] The Side effects of hyperthyroidism include, fatigue, insomnia, heart palpitations, irritability, heat intolerance, increased sweating and the list goes on.[37]

Okay, you are working out, eating a decent diet, and getting to bed on time but the number on the scale and your waistline are steadily increasing. It might be time to have your Thyroid hormone levels tested. With hypothyroidism your body does not produce enough thyroid hormones and your body systems begin to slow down. Many of the symptoms of hypothyroidism are similar to hyperthyroidism but also include weight gain, or difficulty losing weight, and cold intolerance. I began to feel colder when no one else was complaining, my hair was thinning, skin drier and I did not quite have the memory I once enjoyed.

I never had an official diagnosis from my doctor but I again worked with my nutritionist who tweaked my diet and put me on ThyroSense by Women Sense. ThyroSense is a thyroid supplement designed to nourish and support thyroid health. Within a month's time I could definitely feel relief from my symptoms. Again, what's the big to do? Your thyroid gland produces hormones called Triodothyronine (T3) and Tetraiodothyronine, or Thyroxine (T4)[38]. These hormones are the boss of your metabolism and have significant effects on all other body systems. Metabolism translates into how many calories you burn, your body temperature, and your weight. For the women I know these concerns become increasingly important with each passing birthday.

The test for your thyroid is called the TSH which measures your thyroid stimulating hormone levels. It analyzed your bodies T3, T, thyroid panel, and thyroid antibodies.[39] **A healthy or normal range for TSH is between 0.3 and 3.04 with the optimum being a little less than 2.0.**[40] For some women a level above 2.0 may indicate a preclinical or an official diagnosis of hypothyroidism. Hey just check it out.

Many women need to address these issues and many more; but, I will stop here for now. Let me add my disclaimer here. I am not advocating any product or service. I have simply shared my experience and what worked for me. Your health choices are decisions to make with your professional health provider and your family. Just make sure you take care of you and remember the information you provide helps your doctor serve your better. Do not withhold pertinent information and please throw shyness and embarrassment in the trash because; they cannot help you.

Please talk about your health concerns. Talk to your family, talk to your friends and learn what your friends and family are experiencing. Don't automatically assume you have a condition which has not been diagnosed; get accurate info. Talk to your doctor and share your conditions, feelings and family history. It may help them save your life. These conditions are not anything to joke about. My desire was to provide enough information to help you start exploring your own potential issues or concerns. I do know one thing for sure. Our bodies are so wonderfully made of different parts which must work together. If you give your body what it needs, it will heal.

15

Communication

Effective communication is the core of all great relationships, the key word is effective. Productive communication requires the presence of certain conditions and commitments.

In order to bring yourself to the center of an effective conversation you need to recognize your presence is the first step. You must bring yourself and set aside the many other things you could be doing or are still doing mentally. You need to know who you are in the equation, what your needs are, and your communication goal. This does not mean rehearsing exactly what you are going to say to make sure your say it all. It won't hurt to jot down a few concerns as a gentle reminder but not as bullets for your fully loaded magnum.

As true conversation unfolds you may find your concerns and what you need to communicate has changed as you actually listen to what the other person has to say. You should know how you would like the conversation to end, but do not carve it into a script or you may find yourself terribly disappointed.

Communication Building Blocks

Fifty percent of communication is embedded in body language and facial expressions.[1] There are so many elements of communication. To cover all of them adequately, it would take a whole book on this topic alone. I have identified six ingredients, which if practiced, are sure to promote better communication. Communicating is not simply talking to someone; it involves giving, receiving, and processing information together. The building blocks of effective communication are listening, integrity, respect, empathy, clarity, and love.

Listening

The first step in any communication process involves **Listening**. You need to listen to what is being said verbally and non-verbally. You also need to listen to what you are saying verbally and no-verbally. There are times our mouths are speaking about one issue and our bodies are saying something else. You are not simply being quiet to wait your turn to speak, listen to what is being said. Remember we have one mouth and two ears. You should be able to paraphrase what your man has said to you and identify the feelings conveyed.

Integrity
For effective communication, you must have **Integrity**. This means you must be willing to be honest with yourself and your partner about what you are feeling and thinking. Take off the masks and be real and honest. No deceptions or pretty little white lies. Be courageous and tell the truth.

Respect
You must also bring to the conversation **Respect** for yourself and for your partner. Respect will allow you to value the person you are speaking with and their right to their feelings and opinions, while also valuing your own. You do not have to agree about everything to get along. You just need to be willing to understand and work things out. Your opinions and emotions are valued equal. It is what you do with them that reflect a positive or negative intention.

Empathy
Respect will allow you to have **Empathy** for your partner. This empathy means you are willing to imagine what they are feeling, but you are not feeling sorry for them. You are open to how it might feel to walk in their shoes for a moment.

Clarity
Next, you must bring **Clarity**. Simply say what you mean and mean what you say. No guessing games or charades accepted if your true goal is effective communication. Effective communication does not mean you walk away with what you wanted or that one of you wins. Communication is not a battle.

Love
It's all about **Love**. If you show up to communicate with the spirit of love, successful communication is almost guaranteed. Let love guide your choice of words. Be truthful and kind. Remember, our purpose for existence is about relationships and we experience and process relationships through communication. Better communication translates as better relationships. These communication elements are good for all relationships. The question to always consider before you enter important conversations is, "Where is the love?".

Men and Women Communicate Differently
Communication styles are reflections of who we are and how we learned to communicate as children. Women are definitely the talkers and we ask questions to gather information. We also prefer some sort of input or interaction and like to connect with individuals with whom we are speaking with. Through talking things out, we process thoughts, perceive understanding, and responses. Men want the facts. Most men don't want any colorful information or more information than is needed for the situation at hand. Men tend to be compartmentalized thinkers more

like a waffle and your thoughts are boundless more like spaghetti noodles.[2] Men are problem solvers and want to know what is expected of them right up front.

As you consider his communication style and skills, you must keep in mind men are hardwired to be providers and supporters and to meet the needs of family. A man who does not have the desire to provide for his family is not completely whole. A man will also make provisions for the mother of his child even if they were never married or have been divorced. Separated, divorced, or never married men provide for the people who have become his family. Trust me, this is a good thing and you do not want to change this about him. Don't allow the spirit of jealousy to rob you of needed provisions.

You might simply want to share the nuances of your day, but he registers it as a challenge for him to solve or fix. The common thought is women are emotionally-oriented and men are more analytically-focused. He wants to make everything better for you. For the days you really need to talk and he is your only option, you should begin your conversation by letting him know right up front that you do not need him to do anything but listen. Tell him you simply need to vent and all he has to do is listen and maybe nod his head in agreement a time or two. It will allow him to be there for you without the pressure of having to fix you or your problem. Ladies please don't make your man be your girlfriend. You should have girlfriends be your girlfriends.

Communicate what you are feeling and desiring without infusing it with emotional and manipulative tactics you may have learned. Again, say what you mean and mean what you say.

Communicate on the Move

Sometimes men communicate better or easier when in movement or some sort of physical activity. They generally become uncomfortable when we call them to the sit down for face-to-face/eye-to-eye chats we like to have. Their defense goes up and they immediately think they have done something wrong and are in trouble. This is not a good feeling. Do you want to have a non-threatening conversation with your man? Go shoot hoops with him and start talking about real stuff while you are also talking trash about the game, even if you aren't any good at the game. He will be caught off guard and less defensive because he is in his element. It will be a game changer for your relationship and you have more productive communication. If his thing is not basketball, do whatever activity he enjoys, preferably physical and not sexual.

If you cannot participate in a physical activity, then make sure you consider the importance of the effects of warm and accepting touch when approaching sensitive subjects. Back to that touch thing. I do not know a man who does not enjoy the touch of the woman he loves. The more he is touched, the more he will open up to you in conversation. You need to incorporate daily touching not immediately accompanied by sex. Touching during sex is a given and it has a different meaning. For important conversations you need to include caring and supportive non-sexual touch when possible. Touching his hands, arms, or back signals your care non-threatening intentions. We know it is easier to communicate with someone in a common language. You do not have to be fluent in a foreign language to be able to communicate with someone, if you have an understanding of the situation and their needs.

Another communication suggestion is to allow him time to process information and questions. Don't make him give you an on the spot response, with every question. He will often come back with a response later or he will do something to let you know he was listening. Give him space to communicate the best way he knows how. Guys acknowledge communicating with us is often an area of challenge. Since they know we are more skilled in this area we do not have to make them feel bad about it. Also when you are angry and wanting to confront him, remind yourself you do love him and run down a list of a few of the great things about him, which caused you to grow in love with him in the first place.

Just because you are angry, because he did not do something you wanted him to do, or he made a mistake and told you to back away from the table and put the fork down, does not make him the enemy. In not so pretty and excessively heated conventions, I have been compared to being a bull in a china shop. I guess I damaged a whole lot of china. Remember some precious china cannot be replaced or repaired and spoken words cannot be unspoken.

Feeling Words

A major communication challenge for both men and women is being able to identify appropriate words to describe their feelings. If you ask someone what they are feeling, typically they tell you what they are thinking. If you are interested in having your needs met and meeting the needs of others, you will have to learn how to name your feelings most accurately. Feeling words are usually expressed with descriptive verbs and or adjectives. Some feeling words include: appreciative, thankful, touched, grateful, relieved, frightened, scared, sad, aroused, angry, agitated, satisfied, lonely, tired, depressed, hurt, comfortable, hungry, excited, worried, sexy loved rejected, empowered, heard, deceived, etc., and any other sexy words you like to use. Develop a vocabulary of feeling words. It is so much more difficult for a person to become offended or even hurt if you are sincerely and non-judgmentally sharing what you are feeling.

Talking About Sex

Ladies be wary of a gentleman you meet who immediately begins to engage in sexual conversations. If he is expressing sexual thoughts and comments about you, you should not be flattered. This is a huge red flag and you should run away. What is he really telling you? He is telling you he is immature and has not developed an adult level of functioning, allowing him to control and delay gratification. He is impatient and selfish. He is not interested in honoring you as the gift of woman you are. His inability to consciously avoid conversation about sexual fulfillment, places him in an area of arrested development, an early stage of adolescent functioning, like a man-child. It is truly not attractive or edifying in any way.

You know you are attracted to each other or you would not be conversing in the first place. You should focus your conversations on getting to know each other and find out if the attraction contains any substance capable of building the foundation of a healthy relationship. In this order, it will be easier to build and maintain appropriate boundaries. If you indulge in the conversation and feel flattered in any way, you just may end up in bed with him. Don't let this happen, shut it down.

The ability to establish healthy boundaries becomes virtually impossible if you rush into sex. Once you engage in sexual activities with a new person in your life, you immediately lose your abilities to think or make sound decisions. In essence you become stupid regardless of how smart you normally are. You end up sleeping with a stranger. This marks the beginning of sleeping with the enemy. Sex is not love and love is not sex. There will come a time when you need to talk about sex but just wait and get to know the man first. Don't panic, there are some good men out there who value many of the things you value. You will never meet him if you're caught up with Mr. Not Quite Right. And there is an appropriate time to talk about sex… just take your time!

Praise Good Fathers

All men require praise. A good father should be praised for being a good father even though it is his job. Men thrive and flourish in environments which offer sincere praise and appreciation. Women like to be praised too. A man has a need to be praised similar to our needs for affection and attention. You can meet this need. Today, fathers who enjoy fatherhood and who are doing great jobs are often viewed as superheroes. However we should never take the attitude that we do not need to praise him for doing his job.

Heroes need praise too. And those great guys who have not quite reached hero status may get a little closer with the right praise, motivation, and the right words, from the right person. Who does not want to hear they have done a good thing? Those of us who have had this revelation all want to hear, "Well done my good and faithful servant."[3] Real men are energized by the feelings and knowledge they have and can meet the needs of their families, loved ones, or even a stranger in need. This speaks to a man's soul. So let him help you with anything and everything he can. Praise him, touch him, and respect him and he will love you.[4]

Love Languages

Since we are talking about romantic relationships, we need to examine Love Languages. I highly recommend *The Five Love Languages* by author Gary Chapman. All relationships including non-romantic relationships and friendships will benefit from the blessings of this book. For any woman who wants to better understand her partner's most effective preference for receiving love, this is a great place to start. You can refer your partner to read the book as well. In the book, Dr. Chapman introduces the five love languages as: Words of Affirmation, Quality Time, Receiving Gifts, Acts of Service, and Physical Touch.[5] When you have a moment, visit www.5lovelanguages.com and take a brief assessment. You can answer the questions to determine your love language and receive insight, to understand and define how you would like to be loved. Encourage your partner to do the same; the questionnaire will take less than 10 minutes to complete.

If your love language is Words of Affirmation, you are hungry to hear how helpful and needed you are. You need to hear your partner or friends profess their love to you and you crave organic praise and compliments. If Quality Time is your love language, you feel loved when your partner wants to spend time focused on you. You need people to show up for you and give you face time to know you are important to them. Before I read the love language of Receiving Gifts, I thought it was about materialism but it is not. The love language of receiving gifts is about the receiver feeling valued by the givers thoughts and intentions. The gesture of a gift and a perfect gift signal deep affection for this love language. The love language, Acts of Service is energized by services being performed for her or him. Helping around the house, assisting with the planning of important events, and cooking dinner are services which speak to the core of this individual. The love language of Physical Touch is not just about sex. This love language sincerely appreciates hugs, squeezes, back rubs, holding hands, and other forms of thoughtful touch. Touch signifies close proximity and accessibility which translate as love.

Angry Words

It has been said, words spoken in anger are truthful. The more accurate saying was about intoxicated people, "A drunken man never lies." And even this statement is not 100 percent true. A liar is a liar weather drunk or sober. Alcohol is a depressant and it does reduce your natural inhibitions. But that's about it. Okay, so words spoken in anger are definitely hurtful but they do not usually encompass all the truth, of what the person saying the words are actually thinking and feeling. Have you ever spoken in anger only to regret or apologize for your words later? Please do not overvalue words spoken in anger. If you or your partner cannot control your words or language when a conversation heats up, you should defer the conversation to a time in which you can be in more control. It really is that simple. This will become easier if you can maintain a position of assertiveness, which speaks to a positive confidence and not an attacking and offensive stance of aggression.

Stop the Madness

Sisters, we have to stop keying cars, breaking car windows, burning clothes, making a scene at his job, stealing work IDs, and Passports to get back at men who have hurt you. You better know, a few of these offenses are punishable by federal laws. Don't lie to your children about your exes or get them involved in your relationship challenges. Don't use your children to get what you think you want or to keep him from moving forward in a new relationship. Don't hack email addresses, Facebook pages, or spread nasty rumors at his job. Be grateful you have the truth and know you no longer have to be in a loveless relationship. He clearly has not made the best choice and it is his loss. Move on and be the best person you can be. Take advantage of a new start and redefine who you want to be. When you continue to shine and he realizes his poor choice, it will hurt him more than any property or reputation damage you might want to cause him. Will moving on and away from a relationship hurt? YES. The pain of heartbreak is real. It is emotional and physical, but you will survive. Pray, call on your girls, and other supports/support groups you have. If you don't have a support group, it's time to create one.

> *No one can make you feel bad about yourself without your permission.*
> *~Eleanor Roosevelt*

Early Screening: Dante's Baby Mama Drama

In conversation with a young man recently, he told me the relationship with his daughter's mother did not work out because he discovered they were not compatible. In response to this comment, I asked "You were compatible enough to do the wild monkey dance with her, when did you discover you were not compatible?" He laughed. I then asked him to describe what Miss. Compatible looked like, for him. He began by saying, Ms. Compatible would have to like music; she has to have an open mind and she must be spiritual.

There was a pause after this, so I asked him to please continue. He said those were just the basic and foundational things he needed. I explained this was precisely where he went wrong. I told him he stopped with only three things that were so basic and vague. Most people you meet actually meet these qualifications. This information was not specific and significant enough to consider entering into an intimate relationship. Affinity to music, an open mind, and spiritual declaration are not deep qualifiers and definitely do not provide enough information to make a decision about sharing you stuff. We must dig deeper. Questioning a random selection of people in your office, on the metro, or at any social gathering would likely result in a positive response to all three of his compatibility requirements. You must probe and ask questions that will reveal specifics and levels or grades of the qualifiers. When attraction occurs, potential dates appeal to our senses and appear to meet initial criteria. If we are not careful, we will began to give ourselves away without exploring deeper or more authentic character traits.

I know I keep repeating myself, but getting to know someone takes time and attraction is not a sign of compatibility. Character traits necessary for healthy and fulfilling relationships must be observed over time and not simply talked about. If we proceed into relationship based on an affirmative response to Dante's three requirements, relationships become complicated because we begin to give away or share our hearts and bodies with insufficient information. Before we know it, we have become intertwined and entangled in many ways. This is exactly what happened in his situation. His daughter is only a year old. It is a bit late to determine there is a lack of capability. He will be connected to his daughter's mother for the rest of his life. Would it not have been better for him to take time to get to know her before they became sexually involved? Yes!

Sex will always be available. Private parts do not fade away or disappear because you are getting to know someone. Do not rush into sex and do not rush into a relationship for sex. Sex is better with someone you know, love, and trust. Ladies, the truth is we have much more at stake, if the relationship does not work out. Do not set yourself up for the pain of heartbreak, emotional, spiritual, and financial challenges. And if you decide to have sex, please protect yourself. Your health affects everyone in your life directly or indirectly. It is more difficult to back out of something than it is to avoid entering the wrong door or opportunity. Also, remember you have the Stop Loss option discussed earlier. Hear me ladies, we play a part in every situation that presents in our lives. Nothing just simply happens to us.

Mr. Kendall

Ladies please listen to what your Dads say. They really do know what they are talking about. Mr. Kendall is the father of two boys and one girl. I don't know about the conversation he had with his sons, but he shared the precious information, he shared with his daughter. When his daughter came to the appropriate age of dating, he had a conversation with her, to make sure he provided information to help her make smart decisions, when it came to boys. First he told her there would never be another man who would love her as much as he did, as her father. Men would love her differently. Mr. Kendall knew his wife had already had the birds and bees conversation with her and she was a smart young woman. He said, "I know your mother has already talked with you about the biology of sex and taught you how to take care of yourself. But I want you to remember this one thing. When it comes to your virginity, you have the power to give or withhold this gift, and it is a true gift. It is a gift you can only give one time. I would prefer you wait for your husband; but I cannot make that decision for you. So if you do not wait for your husband, if you decide to give this gift to someone before you are married, make sure it is a decision you will not regret later. In years to come, if you run into this person, will you be able to say he is someone you could be proud of or would you be embarrassed to be associated with him? Think very carefully and seriously before you decide to give your gift away. In doing so you will help keep me out of jail for murder." Mr. Kendall's message to his daughter was actually a gift itself and is a beautiful gift to anyone who will accept his advice. Ladies whether it is your first time or if you have been married for 30 years, each time you share yourself with your man; it is a gift that should always be treasured.

One More Thing: Male Hormones

Women do not usually experience menopause before the mid to late 40's. Official menopause is declared by your doctor after you have not had your menstrual cycle for one full year.[6] However, some young women have experienced menopause as early as 22 due to a serious illness, chemical exposure, or a hysterectomy.[7] Age does not automatically determine health conditions for women or men.

Ladies, there is a new discussion about male hormones and the fact men are not exempt from hormonal imbalances. For the same reasons we experience imbalanced hormones including, certain illnesses, poor diet and health, and aging men do also. Andropause is considered the male version of menopause often referred to as Manopause. Manopause happens when a man's testosterone levels drop to lower than health levels.[8]

Symptoms will impact his energy, weight, general health and moods. I placed this information in communication because you know the extra care and tenderness or kindness you require during or around your monthly cycle. Women who are in perimenopause or who have entered official menopause are probably familiar with mood changes that may be difficult if not impossible to control. Hormones are powerful chemicals. If your man is exhibiting any of these symptoms, know there could be many different causes. Check him out but don't tell him what you are thinking! Just help him keep up with annual physicals and suggest that he opts for some preventative screening and testing. While communicating, please extend him the same patience, love, and grace you would like and need to have shown to you. This grace should also be extended for the loss of a job, death in the family, mistakes he has made, or even the feeling of unyielding birthdays.

Ultimately, good communication is about defined flexibility, sincere intentions to accomplish a common goal, research, personality, habits, preferences and learning to detect signs for yourself and your loved ones. If you don't who will?

PART IV

16

Wrap-Up

Dear Sister Readers and Friends:

I just want to take a moment to thank you for allowing me to share our stories and to accompany you on this journey of discovering or redefining your stuff. I hope you will continue the walk and the work since the work never ends. As masterful as we may become with managing our lives we will never arrive at absolute perfection. Accept all of who you are and strive to be the best you can be and this will make you imperfectly perfect.

On our walk together, we explored the different types of relationships with men and women we should avoid. When we cannot avoid them, we can at least limit or control their potentially damaging effects in our lives. Our journey was not only about relationships. We spent some time exploring what is needed to define who we are and who we want to be. By getting to know ourselves better, we can set goals which reflect our true passions and callings. By maintaining healthy boundaries, nourishing our concepts of self-value and self-love and developing spiritual muscles we can have more joy-filled relationships. Developing stress managing strategies and monitoring our health and physical wellness will make sure we can be around to do the work we want to do and really love the people we love. And by committing to an eternal devotion of studying wisdom's advice and building communication skills, we can tell our loved ones we love them today, since tomorrow is not promised to any of us.

You now have more defined pictures of what Unavailable Men, Non-Family Men, and Man-Child Men, Off-Limits Men, Not Ever Men, Dangerous Men and Toxic Friends look like. The Unavailable Men are not available for a new relationship with you because of other relationships, commitments, and obligations. Non-Family Men are not ready for a real family life. The Man-Child Men still have a lot of growing to do. They are not mature or responsible enough for positive adult relationships.

Off-Limits Men are professionals or people in positions who should protect or guide you in non-romantic activities. Not-Ever Men are family members and relatives with whom you should never enter into a romantic or sexual relationship. These inappropriate relationships are damaging to your mental, emotional and spiritual wellbeing. Dangerous Men are not well and are not capable of functioning in healthy relationships. And finally Toxic Friends are not actually friends at all. Their actions speak louder than their words and sometimes their words tell their ugly truths.

Stuff Management Project

Before we go, I would like to invite you to participate in one more activity with me. Consider this your Personal Stuff Management Project (PSMP). I recently completed a two week Direct Sales Training program that was simply amazing. At the end of each learning module and activity, the facilitator required all participants to "teach back" to the class what we just learned. You cannot teach what you don't know; however, if you can teach any subject to someone else, it means you have comprehended the material and know it well enough to teach it. In addition, teaching has a way of solidifying your new and existing knowledge because you have to add structure and also be able to articulate and communicate what you know.

Back in chapter 11 when we covered boundaries, I asked you to write letters to yourself and others about forgiveness, and in chapter six, you wrote a letter to your younger self. These letters will be helpful for this exercise, so pull it out. Also, I would like you to review your journal reflection entries, at the end of each chapter. Once you have completed this review, go back and visit any of the stories that spoke to you because you either had a similar experience, know someone else who had a similar experience or simply felt the pain experienced in the stories.

Now that you have reviewed your journal entries and progress notes, I would like you to create some form of presentation about all the things you learned on this walk with me. Please infuse your presentation with your own stories and examples. Offer visual aids by using Word or PowerPoint applications, poster boards, puppets, animation, or whatever your imagination can conceive and create. There are many movies and movie clips which can provide examples, discussion material, and resources for your presentation. Allow your creativity and passion to flow.

When you have completed your project, I challenge you to first share it with some close friends and family. After sharing with them and receiving their feedback, I challenge you to go on and share it with the leaders of the teens, young adults and single's ministries at your church. If you are uncomfortable with this option try a local women's support group, shelter, or rehabilitation program. If the first two options do not appeal to you, I plead with you to gather a few of the young ladies you know and bless them with what you know about the issues and challenges we covered. If your process is still too sensitive or you feel it too personal to share for whatever reasons, you must know you are not being judged; but you still can help another. You can help even while still processing your own experiences. Finally, if you cannot tell your story simply gather a few young ladies in your neighborhood and share with them the Relationship Preparedness System (RPS) which consists of the First Three Steps and the LOAV Method. You can also walk them through goal setting and the Personal Forgiveness Project without sharing any of your experiences. Break it down and make it as plain as you possibly can. If you can only complete this option, you will be credited with a great act of service.

Use this Personal Stuff Management Project to impact and empower the young ladies and women in your neighborhoods and communities. I have set up a site where you can find additional support and share your events and success stories. www.LoveSpeaks2u.com/blog.html. The information you share will help your fellow sisters make better life decisions. Not only will you help guide and shape lives you will also save a few. You just never know who you are talking to and what their experiences have been. I am empowering you to go forward and speak life and speak love from one sister to another.

It has been an absolute pleasure and honor to journey with you. I look forward to hearing your stories and your victories. Please remember, in all the circumstances in your life, if you are seeking true love, you will find him right in the middle.

Love always,

Princess Love Mills

17

Final Reflections

DON'T JUST GIVE YOUR STUFF AWAY

Listen up Baby Girl; I've got something to say
Don't just give your stuff away
I say don't just give your stuff away
I say don't just give your stuff away
Back up!

Real friends treat your well
Your secrets they will not tell

Good boyfriends don't cause you pain
They don't treat you like a pet they to train

It doesn't matter if you're a girl or a boy
I won't become your play toy

My time is extremely valuable
Before I share I need to know if we're compatible

I know who I am and I like myself
I know that prosperity is more than wealth

You cannot buy me with your dollars
Or with your fancy cars, lies and white collars

You see the agents who work for me have wings
And they reveal your secrete things
Like your girlfriend
Your wife
Your three kids
Your baby mama
You can keep the drama
Because I'm managing my stuff

I'm the President and the CEO
You can't come close unless I say so

You see, I'm more than just a pretty face
I have dominion in this place

All you see belongs to me
And I am the one who holds the key
To my heart, my mind
My money, my time

My heart, my mind
My body, it's all mine
I'm managing my stuff

Listen up Baby Girl do you hear what I say?
Don't just give your stuff away
I say don't just give your stuff away
I say don't just give your stuff away
Back up

You have to manage your own stuff
Delegating will not be enough

You have to know your bottom line
Because not ever offer is intended to be kind

You are the Queen who sits on the throne
You are the boss of your own home

The battle is won and lost in the mind
You have to know that you're one of a kind

You are beautiful and wonderfully made
There is absolutely nothing worthy of your trade

You are worth more than your weight in gold
You keep divinity from the cold

So take my advice and join with me
It will ensure that you will always be free
Learn the art of managing your heart
This small act will make you truly smart

I'm managing my stuff
My heart, my mind
My money, my time

My heart, my mind
My body, it's all mine

FINAL REFLECTION

Stuff management, I'm managing my stuff

If you keep it real and keep it true
I just might share my stuff with you

But if you want to break me down and make me feel blue
I know exactly what to do with you

My heart will not settle for almost right
One thing I've learned with my stuff is how to fight

I will not be shy and I will not be coy
I have learned to harness and manage my joy

I will not settle for your being your lover
And I certainly don't want to become your mother

You see I require a real man who can stand up for me
One who will make sure that I remain free

He will not put me in a cage
Or subject me to any kind of rage

I will not have to compete for his affection
Because we will have a deep loyal connection

He will love me and treat me right
And the candles or our love will always shine bright

If you cannot prove that you're worthy of my treasures
Then for you I will not give any of my pleasures

I've had some lessons and some were quire hard
This is why my heart will remain under guard

I'm sharing this message and hope that you will learn
Ladies with the right man, you don't have to wait for your turn

The universal understanding of the word respect
Will keep you from feeling the meaning of neglect

Learn to respect and honor yourself
And begin to investment in your internal wealth

It's called Stuff Management. Learn to manage your stuff

Notes

Introduction
1. Cambridge Editorial Partnership. (2006). The greatest American speeches: The stories and transcripts of the words that changed our history. "Ain't I a woman?" London: Quercus Publishing Ltd. (p. 41)

Chapter 1- What is "Your Stuff"?
1. Harvey, Steve (2009). Act like a lady, think like a man: What men really think about love, relationships, intimacy, and commitment. New York: Amistad Collins Publishing
2. Shange, Ntozake (1977). For colored girls who have considered suicide, when the rainbow is enuf: a choreopoem. New York: Scribner Poetry.
3. Ibid.
4. Genesis 2:18: The LORD God said, "It is not good for the man to be alone. I will make a helper suitable for him."
5. Harvard Health Publications. December 2010. "The Health Benefits of Strong Relationships" http://www.health.harvard.edu/newsletters/Harvard_Womens_Health_Watch/2010/December/the-health-benefits-of-strong-relationships. Accessed October 2012.
6. Ibid
7. Harvard Health Publications. January 18, 2011. "Strengthen Relationships for Longer, Healthier Life." http://www.health.harvard.edu/healthbeat/strengthen-relationships-for-longer-healthier-life. Accessed October 2012.
8. Philippians 4:13: I can do all this through him who gives me strength.
9. Proverbs 4:23: Above all else, guard your heart, for everything you do flows from it.
10. Ibid
11. Job 22:28: What you decide on will be done, and light will shine on your ways.
12. Proverbs 18:21: The tongue has the power of life and death, and those who love it will eat its fruit.
13. Psalm 139:14: I praise you because I am fearfully and wonderfully made; your works are wonderful,
    I know that full well.

Chapter 2- The Lists
1. Genesis 2:7: Then the LORD God formed a man from the dust of the ground and breathed into his nostrils the breath of life, and the man became a living being. Job 33:4: The Spirit of God has made me; the breath of the Almighty gives me life.

Chapter 3- Unavailable Men
1. Webster's Dictionary Online. 2012. http://dictionary.reference.com/browse/unavailable?s=t
2. Harvey, Steve (2009). Act like a lady, think like a man: What men really think about love, relationships, intimacy, and commitment. New York: Amistad Collins Publishing
3. Calvin Jordan, February 10, 2011 Conversation
4. Romans 12:2: Do not conform to the pattern of this world, but be transformed by the renewing of your mind. Then you will be able to test and approve what God's will is—his good, pleasing and perfect will.

Grayson
1. "What's Love Got to do with it?" by Tina Turner
2. Rowena Nibert, April, 2012 Conversation

NOTES

Toby
1. Psalms 18:35: You make your saving help my shield, and your right hand sustains me; your help has made me great.
2. Isaiah 38: 2-5: Hezekiah turned his face to the wall and prayed to the LORD, 3 "Remember, Lord, how I have walked before you faithfully and with wholehearted devotion and have done what is good in your eyes." And Hezekiah wept bitterly. 4 Then the word of the Lord came to Isaiah: 5 "Go and tell Hezekiah, 'This is what the Lord, the God of your father David, says: I have heard your prayer and seen your tears; I will add fifteen years to your life.
3. Hebrews 4:16: Let us then approach God's throne of grace with confidence, so that we may receive mercy and find grace to help us in our time of need.
4. Acts 2:21: And everyone who calls on the name of the Lord will be saved.
5. T. D. Jakes Ministries. Sunday, April 15, 2012 Save the Scraps Part I. http://www.lightsource.com/ministry/the-potters-house/save-the-scraps-part-1-270557.html
6. Luke 11:9: "So I say to you: Ask and it will be given to you; seek and you will find; knock and the door will be opened to you."

Chapter 4 - Non-Family Men
1. Genesis 9:7: As for you, be fruitful and increase in number; multiply on the earth and increase upon it.
2. "Papa Rollin Stone" by The Temptations

Chapter 7 - Not-EVER Men
1. Leviticus 20: 11-21
2. Morgan, Patrick. February 11, 2011. "Genetic Testing Brings Up a Surprising Topic: Incest" Discover Magazine http://blogs.discovermagazine.com/80beats/2011/02/11/genetic-testing-brings-up-a-surprising-topic-incest/
3. Ibid.
4. Proverbs 27:17: As iron sharpens iron, so one person sharpens another.
5. Romans 12: 10: Be devoted to one another in love. Honor one another above yourselves.
6. Philippians 1:10: so that you may be able to discern what is best and may be pure and blameless for the day of Christ,
7. Philippians 1: 10: so that you may be able to discern what is best and may be pure and blameless for the day of Christ,
8. Meyer, Joyce "Abuse and the Miracle of Recovery." http://www.joycemeyer.org/Articles/ea.aspx?article=abuse_and_the_miracle_of_recovery. Accessed June 2012.
9. King, Deborah. (2009) Truth that heals. What you hide can hurt you. United States: Hay House
10. Ibid.

Chapter 8 - Dangerous Men
1. Kanel, K. (2007). A guide to crisis intervention. (3rd. ed.). Belmont, CA: Brooks/Cole.
2. Women Against Abuse. Types of Domestic Violence. http://www.womenagainstabuse.org/index.php/learn-about-abuse/types-of-domestic-violenceOther issues with relationship abuse
3. Ibid.
4. Ibid.
5. Ibid
6. Rape, Abuse, & Incest National Network. "Who are the Victims?" http://www.rainn.org/get-information/statistics/sexual-assault-victims. Accessed July, 2012
7. See note 2 above.
8. Kopala, M., & Keitel, M. A. (Eds.). (2003). Handbook of counseling women. London: Sage.
9. Ibid.
10. Ibid.

Chapter 9 - Toxic Friendships
1. Couric, K., Katie's Take October 30, 2012 Surviving a http://news.yahoo.com/blogs/katies-take-abc-news/surviving-friend-breakup-112745962.html . Tue, Oct 30, 2012 3:00 AM EDT - ABC News 4:18
2. Ibid
3. Ibid
4. Ibid
5. Luke 10:1: After this the Lord appointed seventy-two others and sent them two by two ahead of him to every town and place where he was about to go.
6. Matthew 10:1: Jesus called his twelve disciples to him and gave them authority to drive out impure spirits and to heal every disease and sickness.
7. Mark 9:2: After six days Jesus took Peter, James and John with him and led them up a high mountain, where they were all alone. There he was transfigured before them.

Chapter 10 - Attachment Styles
1. McLeod, Saul, (2007). "Bowlby's Attachment Theory." Simply Psychology. http://www.simplypsychology.org/bowlby.html. Accessed September 2011.
2. Ibid.
3. Ibid.
4. Ibid.
5. Clinton, T., & Sibcy, G., (2002). Attachments: Why you love, feel, and act the way you do. Brentwood, TN: Thomas Nelson Publishers
6. Ibid
7. Ibid.
8. Ibid.

Chapter 11- Relationship Boundaries
1. Cloud, H., & Towsend, J., (1999). Boundaries in marriage. Grand Rapids, MI: Zondervan.
2. Ibid.
3. Ibid.
4. Ibid.
5. Ibid.
6. Ibid,
7. Ibid.
8. Kornstein, S. G., & Clayton, A. H., (2002). Women's mental health: A comprehensive textbook. New York: The Guilford Press.
9. Psalm 23: 6: Surely your goodness and love will follow me all the days of my life
10. Luke 1: 28: The angel went to her and said, "Greetings, you who are highly favored! The Lord is with you."
11. Isaiah 60:1-3. The Spirit of the Sovereign LORD is on me, because the LORD has anointed me to proclaim good news to the poor. He has sent me to bind up the brokenhearted, to proclaim freedom for the captives and release from darkness for the prisoners, [2] to proclaim the year of the LORD's favor and the day of vengeance of our God, to comfort all who mourn, [3] and provide for those who grieve in Zion to bestow on them a crown of beauty instead of ashes.
12. Ibid.
13. Ecclesiastes 3:1: There is a time for everything, and a season for every activity under the heavens

Chapter 12- Managing Stress & Emotions
1. What is Stress? The American Institute of Stress. http://www.stress.org/what-is-stress/ Accessed October 2011.
2. Greenberg, B. (2006). Fight, Flight, or Breathing Right: The Choice Is Yours. Psych Central. http://psychcentral.com/lib/2006/fight-flight-or-breathing-right-the-choice-is-yours/ Accessed October 2011.
3. Engin, D., (2006). Relationships Among Coping With Stress, Life Satisfaction, Decision Styles, and decision Self-Esteem: an Investigation with Turkish university Students. Society for Personality Research, Inc. 2006.
4. Mayo Clinic Staff. Heart disease in women: Understand symptoms and risk factors. http://www.mayoclinic.com/health/heart-disease/HB00040. Accessed October 2011.
5. Ibid.
6. Collingwood, J. (2007). The Physical Effects of Long-Term Stress. Psych Central. http://psychcentral.com/lib/2007/the-physical-effects-of-long-term-stress/ Accessed October 2011
7. Abdel-Khalvek, A.M., (2006). Measuring happiness with a Single-Item Scale.Society for Personality Research, Inc. 2006.
8. Styhre, A., (2002). Emotional Management and Stress: Managing Ambiguities. Walter de Gruyter and Co. www.findarticles.com/p/articles
9. Ibid
10. http://www.ninds.nih.gov/disorders/brain_basics/understanding_sleep.htm#Tips
11. Ibid.
12. Ibid.
13. Zelman, Kathleen. Benefits of Exercise. WebMD December 9, 2004. http://www.medicinenet.com/benefits_of_exercise/article.htm. Accessed October 2012
14. See note 8 above.
15. US Department of Agriculture. Choose My Plate http://www.choosemyplate.gov/
16. Ibid.
17. Teta, J., (2005). The Impact of Lifestyle Choices and Hormonal Balance on Coping with Stress. The Townsend Letter Group, 2005.
18. Avoron, J., LaValley, M., Solomon, D., Wang, P., & Warsi, A. (2004). Self-Management Education Programs in Chronic Disease: A systematic Review and Methodological Critique Arch Intern Med vol. 164. August 2004. www.archintermed.com
19. 1 Corinthians 6:19: Do you not know that your bodies are temples of the Holy Spirit, who is in you, whom you have received from God? You are not your own;
20. Crowe, Monica. August 21, 2011. How Many Days Can You Survive without Food? Livestrong.com: http://www.livestrong.com/article/523013-how-many-days-can-you-survive-without-food/#EgIxemis. Accessed May 2012
21. Ogunjimi, Angela. Jul 17, 2011. How Long Can the Average Human Go Without Water? Livestrong.com: http://www.livestrong.com/article/494958-how-long-can-the-average-human-go-without-water/ Accessed May 2012
22. Repays, Steve. eHow. How. Long Can Your Brain Survive Without Oxygen? http://www.ehow.com/about_5506985_long-can-brain-survive-oxygen.html#ixzz2EgWqXDVW. Accessed 2012.
23. Ibid.
24. Ibid.
25. Ibid.
26. Ibid.
27. Mayo Clinic: Stress Management. Stress management: Identify your sources of stress. Mayo Clinic. http://www.mayoclinic.com/health/stress-management/SR00031 Accessed September 2012.
28. Mindfulness Gross, S. (2006). Relaxation and Caring For Yourself. Psych Central. Accessed September 2012.
29. See note 18 above.

Chapter 13 - Prayer
1. John 14:15: If you love me, keep my commands.
2. Matthew 11:30: For my yoke is easy and my burden is light.
3. (KJV). 1 John 4: 7-8: "Beloved, let us love one another; for Love is of God, and everyone that loveth is born of God, and knoweth God. He that loveth not knoweth not God; for God is Agape."
4. Luke 15: 12-13: The younger one said to his father, 'Father, give me my share of the estate.' So he divided his property between them.13 "Not long after that, the younger son got together all he had, set off for a distant country and there squandered his wealth in wild living.
5. Luke 15:20: But while he was still a long way off, his father saw him and was filled with compassion for him; he ran to his son, threw his arms around him and kissed him.
6. 1 Corinthians 6:20: Do you not know that your body is a temple of the Holy Spirit, who is in you, whom you have received from God? You are not your own;
7. (KLV). Jeremiah 3:14 Turn, O backsliding children, saith the LORD; for I am married unto you.
8. http://dictionary.reference.com/browse/Backslider
9. http://www.merriam-webster.com/dictionary/backslide
10. Isaiah 46: 10 I make known the end from the beginning, from ancient times, what is still to come. I say: My purpose will stand, and I will do all that I please.
11. 1 John 3:20: For God is greater than our hearts, and he knows everything.
12. Romans 8:38-39: For I am convinced that neither death nor life, neither angels nor demons, neither the present nor the future, nor any powers, neither height nor depth, nor anything else in all creation, will be able to separate us from the love of God that is in Christ Jesus our Lord.
13. John 15:16: You did not choose me, but I chose you and appointed you so that you might go and bear fruit—fruit that will last—and so that whatever you ask in my name the Father will give you.

Chapter 14 - Health & Wellness
1. Kalk, M., 2006. Education.com. Cells, Tissues, and Organs Study Guide. http://www.education.com/study-help/article/cells-tissues-organs/ . Accessed September 2012.
2. Ibid.
3. Ibid
4. American Heart Association July 17 2012 Understanding Blood Pressure Readings: http://www.heart.org/HEARTORG/Conditions/HighBloodPressure/AboutHighBloodPressure/Understanding-Blood-Pressure-Readings_UCM_301764_Article.jsp
5. Ibid.
6. Weil, A., (2006). Eight weeks to optimum health: A proven program for taking full advantage of your body's natural healing power. New Yore: Ballantine Books.
7. Ibid.
8. Pick, M., April 20, 2011.Women to Women. Blood pressure readings - taking your vital signs. http://www.womentowomen.com/hypothyroidism/testing.aspx. Accessed September 22, 2012
9. Ibid.
10. Ibid.
11. Ibid.
12. Ibid.
13. Ibid.
14. I Mayo Clinic September 21, 2012. Cholesterol levels: What numbers should you aim for? http://www.mayoclinic.com/health/cholesterol-levels/CL00001. Accessed September 2012
15. Ibid
16. Ibid
17. Ibid
18. Good vs. bad cholesterol. American Heart Association. http://www.heart.org/HEARTORG/Conditions/Cholesterol/AboutCholesterol/Good-vs-Bad-Cholesterol_UCM_305561_Article.jsp. Accessed September 2012.
19. Ibid

NOTES

20. Ibid
21. Ibid.
22. Ibid
23. Ibid
24. America Diabetes Association. Diabetes Basics; Facts about type 2 http://www.diabetes.org/diabetes-basics/type-2/. Accessed September 2012.
25. Ibid.
26. Ibid.
27. Ibid.
28. Ibid.
29. Ibid.
30. Ibid.
31. National Institute of Health. Office of Dietary Supplements. http://ods.od.nih.gov/factsheets/VitaminD-HealthProfessional/
32. Ibid.
33. Zeratsky, K., July 20, 2012 What are the risks of a vitamin D dificency? Mayo Clinic. http://www.mayoclinic.com/health/vitamin-d-deficiency/AN02182 . Accessed September 2012
34. Ibid.
35. Ibid.
36. Hypothyroidism. The American Thyroid Association. http://www.thyroid.org/what-is-hypothyroidism. Accessed September. 22, 2012
37. Hyperthyroidism. The American Thyroid Association. http://www.thyroid.org/what-is-hyperthyroidism. Accessed September 22, 2012
38. Pick, Marcelle. May 27, 2011.Women to Women. Thyroid testing for hypothyroidism. http://www.womentowomen.com/hypothyroidism/testing.aspx. Accessed September 22, 2012
39. Lab Tests Online. http://labtestsonline.org/understanding/analytes/tsh/tab/test accessed September 22, 2012
40. See note 38 above.

Chapter 15 - Communication

1. Miller, R., & Perlman, D., & Stephens-Brehm, S. (2009). Intimate relationships (5th ed.) New York, New York: McGraw-Hill.
2. Farrel, B & Farrel, P., (2007). Men are like waffles, women are like spaghetti: Understanding and delighting in your differences. Eugene: Harvest House Publishers.
3. Matthew 25:21: Well done, good and faithful servant! You have been faithful with a few things; I will put you in charge of many things. Come and share your master's happiness!
4. Ephesians 5:25: Husbands, love your wives, just as Christ loved the church and gave himself up for he. Colossians 3:19: Husbands, love your wives and do not be harsh with them
5. Chapman, Gary (2010). The five love languages: The secret to love that lasts. Chicago: North Field Publishing.
6. The Boston Women's Health Book Collective Boston University School of Public Health (2005). Our bodies, ourselves: A new edition for a new era. New York: Simon & Schuster
7. Ibid.
8. Ratini, M. June 29, 2012. Male Menopause. Web MD. http://men.webmd.com/guide/male-menopause

Made in the USA
Lexington, KY
30 July 2013